UNITED STATES

COMMISSION ON CIVIL RIGHTS

PERFORMANCE AND ACCOUNTABILITY REPORT (PAR)

FOR FISCAL YEAR 2016

Table of Contents

Section I: Management Discussion and Analysis 1

A. USCCR Mission 1

B. USCCR Organizational Structure 1

    i.   Headquarters Organization 2

    ii.   Regional Programs 4

C. Performance Highlights 6

D. Federal Managers' Financial Integrity Act (FMFIA) 7

E. Financial Highlights 8

F. Limitations on Financial Statements 10

G. Management Statement of Assurance 11

Section II: Performance Report 13

A. Reliability of Performance Data 13

B. Strategic Goal A: The Commission will function as an effective civil rights watchdog and conduct studies and issue publications on important issues of civil rights. 13

    i.   Briefings 14

    ii.   Commission Reports 16

C. Strategic Goal B: The Commission will regularly provide new, objective information and analysis on civil rights issues. 21

D. Strategic Goal C: The Commission will cooperate, where appropriate, with other federal agencies to apprise individuals of civil rights laws and policies and to raise public awareness of civil rights. 22

    i.   Clearinghouse Website 23

    ii.   Complaint Referral Program 23

E. Strategic Goal D: Improve the Commission's profile and effectiveness in communicating with the general public 24

    i.   Press List 25

    ii.   Press Releases 25

    iii. Website Improvements 26

    iv. Speaking Engagements 26

F. Strategic Goal E: Continue to strengthen the Commission's financial and operational controls and advance the Commission's mission through management excellence, efficiency, and accountability. 27

G. Strategic Goal F: Increase the participation of our State Advisory Committees (SACs) in the Commission's work. 28

i.   State Advisory Committee Charters and Appointments 29

ii.   State Advisory Committee Reports 30

iii.   SAC Fact Finding Activity 34

F. Other Information Related to Annual Performance Reporting 35

Section: III: Auditors Report and Financial Statements 36

A. Message from the Chief of Budget and Finance 36

B. Auditor's Report, Financial Statements & Notes 37

Section: IV: Other Accompanying Information 68

A. Summary of Financial Statement Audit and Management Assurances 68

B. Improper Payments Information Act Reporting Details 69

APPENDICES 70

Appendix A: Strategic Plan Goals, Objectives, and Measures 70

Appendix B: FY 2016 Annual Performance Plan, Targets, and Results 79

MESSAGE FROM THE CHAIRMAN

I am pleased to present the annual Performance and Accountability Report (PAR) for the U.S. Commission on Civil Rights for Fiscal Year 2016. This report reflects the agency's program and financial accomplishments over the past year. We received a qualified opinion on our Financial Statements.

In FY 2016, the Commission continued to deliver quality civil rights programming, studies, policy analysis, and recommendations to the President, Congress, and the Nation on important civil rights issues of the day. To promote public awareness of current civil rights laws, remedies, and enforcement agencies, we held four successful briefings: Public Education Funding Inequality in an Era of Increasing Concentration of Poverty and Resegregation; Quiet Crisis: Federal Funding and Unmet Needs in Indian Country, 2016 Update; Environmental Justice: Toxic Materials, Poor Economies; and the Impact on the Environment of Low-Income, Minority Communities; and Municipal Policing and Courts: A Search for Justice or a Quest for Revenue.

In addition to our four briefings, the Commission released three reports. The *Increasing Compliance with Section 7 of the National Voter Registration Act* report examines state compliance with the National Voter Registration Act's mandate to provide voter registration forms and assistance to those utilizing public assistance and disability agencies, and the efforts of the Department of Justice and private citizens in enforcing the mandate, found in Section 7 of the Act. The *Peaceful Coexistence: Reconciling Nondiscrimination Principles with Civil Liberties* report examined the balance struck by federal courts, foremost among them the U.S. Supreme Court, in adjudicating claims for religious exemptions from otherwise applicable nondiscrimination law. Our statutory report, *Environmental Justice: Examining the Environmental Protection Agency's Compliance and Enforcement of Title VI and Executive Order 12,898* examines whether the Environmental Protection Agency ("EPA") is complying with its environmental justice obligations. The Commission heard testimony from the EPA, experts and scholars in the field, and a majority of the Commission made findings and recommendations.

We continue to enhance our engagement with and utilize the work of our state advisory committees. Our state advisory committee members, working with regional office staff, held 11 civil rights briefings and forums. In addition, state advisory committees published nine reports. Over the course of FY 2016, I have been pleased in my capacity as Chair of the Commission to attend meetings of some of our State Advisory Committees and to meet with representatives of state civil and human rights agencies, community groups, civil rights advocates, and public officials regarding the work of the Commission and the civil rights challenges facing diverse communities.

We continue to be challenged by staff vacancies and limited resources. Despite the challenges we face as an agency, I am proud of the Commission's FY 2016 performance, and look forward to building on its performance to continue to advance civil rights through objective and comprehensive investigation, research, and analysis on issues of fundamental concern to the federal government and the public.

Martin R. Castro
Chairperson
United States Commission on Civil Rights
November 15, 2016

Section I: Management Discussion and Analysis

The Management Discussion and Analysis (MD&A) section explains our mission, describes our organizational structure, presents performance highlights, analyzes our internal control environment, identifies financial highlights, and discusses the limitation of financial statements.

A. USCCR Mission

The U.S. Commission on Civil Rights was created pursuant to the Civil Rights Act of 1957, which was signed into law by President Eisenhower. [1] Since then, Congress has reauthorized or extended the legislation creating the Commission several times; the last reauthorization was in 1994 by the Civil Rights Commission Amendments Act of 1994. [2] Established as an independent, bipartisan, fact-finding federal agency, our mission is to appraise the development of national civil rights policy and enhance enforcement of federal civil rights laws. We pursue this mission by studying alleged deprivations of voting rights and alleged discrimination based on race, color, religion, sex, age, disability, or national origin, or in the administration of justice. We play a vital role in advancing civil rights through objective and comprehensive investigation, research, and analysis on issues of fundamental concern to the federal government and the public.

B. USCCR Organizational Structure

The Commission is an independent federal agency led by eight appointed commissioners. Their responsibilities include establishing agency policy on civil rights issues; adopting program plans, goals, and priorities; and approving national office project proposals. The staff director, appointed by the President with the concurrence of a majority of the commissioners, is the administrative head of the agency. The organizational chart below shows our current structure.

---

[1]Civil Rights Act of 1957, Pub. L. No. 85-315, § 101, 71 Stat. 634 (1957). See United States Commission on Civil Rights Act of 1983, Pub. L. No. 98-183, 97 Stat. 1301 (1983); United States Commission on Civil Rights Act of 1991, Pub. L. No. 102-167, ___ Stat. ___ (1991).
[2]Civil Rights Commission Amendments Act of 1994, Pub. L. No. 103-419, 108 Stat. 4338 (1994) (codified at 42 U.S.C.A. § 1975 (2005)).

Organizational Structure

U.S. Commission on Civil Rights

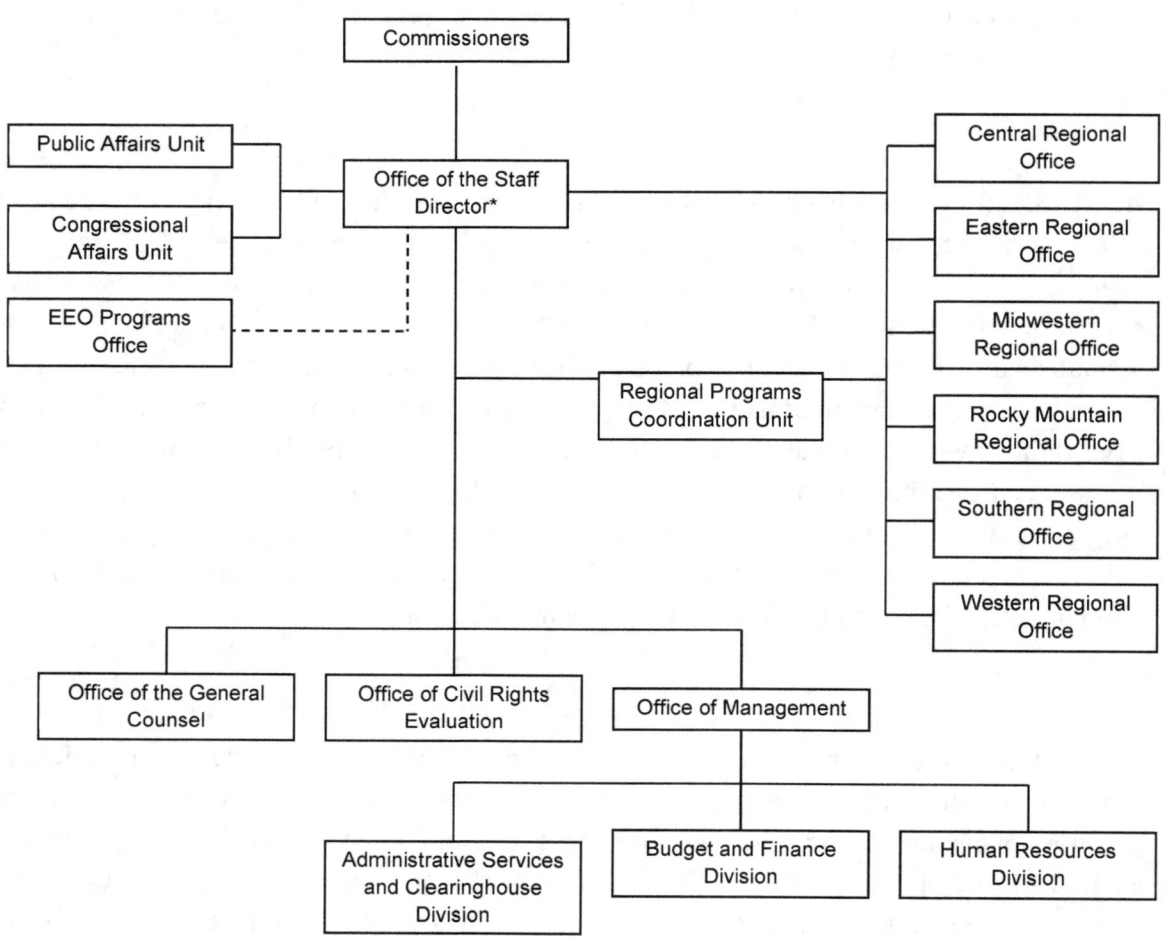

* Although current agency regulations describe an "Office of the Deputy Staff Director," the Commission eliminated that office and the deputy staff director position has been transferred to the Office of the Staff Director.

i.   **Headquarters Organization**

There are eight offices and units in our national office and six regional offices. Of the national offices, two are primarily responsible for civil rights-related research and study—the Office of Civil Rights Evaluation and the Office of the General Counsel. Descriptions of the key functions for each office and unit are below.

Office of the Staff Director

The Office of the Staff Director (OSD), through the staff director, oversees the overall operation and management of our agency including:

- disseminating policies established by the commissioners to staff;
- recommending program activities and projects for approval by the commissioners,
- managing agency-wide performance and evaluating program results;
- overseeing and coordinating the completion of the agency's substantive civil rights work;
- ensuring that the budget is executed in a manner consistent with established agency priorities; and
- serving as the liaison between the Commission and the Executive Office of the President, Congress, and other federal agencies.

Office of the General Counsel

The Office of the General Counsel (OGC) provides the legal expertise and advice required to support our fact-finding and ensure the legal integrity of our written products. This office supports the lawful operation of the agency and advises agency leadership and managers on a range of legal matters. This may include analyzing proposed legislation, interpreting various laws and regulations, advising on the scope of the agency's jurisdiction, and representing the agency in contractual disputes. The general counsel and his or her staff also represent the agency in personnel matters including litigation arising from equal employment discrimination complaints and other alleged employment violations. In addition, this office develops concepts for briefings and hearings on civil rights issues and generates related reports for public dissemination.

Office of Civil Rights Evaluation

The Office of Civil Rights Evaluation (OCRE) provides the subject matter and analytical expertise required to prepare social-scientific evaluations of civil rights issues. This office monitors the activities of numerous federal agencies as well as national and regional civil rights trends. Based on information gathered through monitoring and other sources, this office develops concepts for, and conducts, civil rights studies and other projects. In addition to these functions, this office receives, reviews, and refers civil rights complaints to other agencies for appropriate enforcement action.

Office of Management

The Office of Management (OM) supports all of the agency's strategic goals and objectives by ensuring that human and financial capital are available, and administrative support is in place to achieve the agency's mission. The OM provides administrative support to all other

Commission offices. Several divisions fall within this office: the Budget and Finance Division, the Human Resources Division, and the Administrative Services and Clearinghouse Division. The Administrative Services and Clearinghouse Division is responsible for information technology, procurement and acquisition, copying, printing, mail and distribution services, and the Rankin National Civil Rights Library.

Congressional Affairs Unit

The Congressional Affairs Unit (CAU) serves as our liaison with Congress, responding to requests for specific information, identifying opportunities for our commissioners and others to provide testimony and information to congressional members and their staff on civil rights matters, and ensuring the distribution of our studies and reports to all members. CAU monitors the legislative activities of Congress and provides support in the conceptualization and production of studies and reports with information gathered via its monitoring activities. All staff positions in CAU are vacant. The public affairs unit performs the essential responsibilities of the congressional and public affairs units.

Public Affairs Unit

The Public Affairs Unit (PAU) serves as the public voice of the Commission and ensures that the public knows about our activities and publications. It is also responsible for coordinating and carrying out such activities as briefing reporters, holding press conferences, issuing press releases, arranging press interviews and speaking engagements for commissioners and approved staff, and monitoring press activity regarding the Commission and civil rights issues. PAU deals directly with the public in responding to inquiries and by attending meetings of civil rights organizations.

Equal Employment Opportunity Programs

The Equal Employment Opportunity (EEO) Programs office is responsible for the overall management of our equal employment opportunity compliance system. This system provides a means of review and appeal for applicants for employment and employees of the Commission, who believe that they were victims of discrimination based on race, color, age, religion, national origin, sex (including sexual harassment), physical or mental disability, or reprisal in connection with EEO-related activities. All staff positions in CAU are vacant.

ii.   **Regional Programs**

Regional Programs Coordination Unit

The chief of the Regional Programs Coordination Unit (RPCU) supervises the activities of the Commission's six regional offices. The chief of RPCU is responsible for coordinating, monitoring, and reporting on regional activities for the national office, and communicating national office policies and priorities to regional offices. The chief of RPCU also serves as the agency's Committee Management Officer (CMO) regarding the agency's public reporting under the Federal Advisory Committee Act (FACA) on its 51 state advisory committees.

<u>Regional Offices: Organization and State Alignment</u>

The six regional offices provide critical support to the 51 state advisory committees required by our statute. A regional director leads each office and generally has one administrative assistant. These offices coordinate the Commission's operations in their regions and assist the state advisory committees in their activities. Regional directors are also responsible for the day-to-day administration of their office and the supervision of office staff.

Presented below is our regional alignment.

- Central Region (CRO): Alabama, Arkansas, Iowa, Kansas, Louisiana, Mississippi, Missouri, Nebraska, and Oklahoma.
- Eastern Region (ERO): Connecticut, Delaware, District of Columbia, Maine, Maryland, Massachusetts, New Hampshire, New Jersey, New York, Pennsylvania, Rhode Island, Vermont, Virginia, and West Virginia.
- Western Region (WRO): Alaska, Arizona, California, Hawaii, Idaho, Nevada, Oregon, Texas, and Washington.
- Southern Region (SRO): Florida, Georgia, Kentucky, North Carolina, South Carolina, and Tennessee.
- Rocky Mountain Region (RMRO): Colorado, Montana, New Mexico, North Dakota, South Dakota, Utah, and Wyoming.
- Midwestern Region (MWRO): Illinois, Indiana, Michigan, Minnesota, Ohio, and Wisconsin.

This subsection highlights our performance during the fiscal year. We exceeded, substantially met, or met 71 percent of our performance targets. The pie chart represents our overall level of performance for the year.

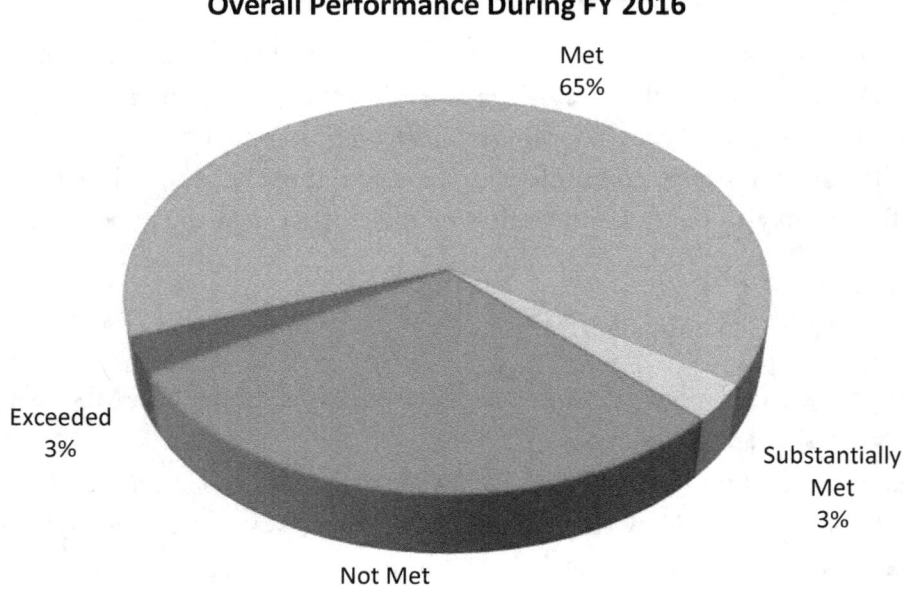

Overall Performance During FY 2016

While we faced staffing and management constraints, we were able to meet or exceed most of our goals.

A detailed discussion of each strategic goal, its FY 2016 target performance, and our actual performance are in the section titled "Section II: Performance Report." A comparison of agency performance for the last three years is presented in the below bar chart.

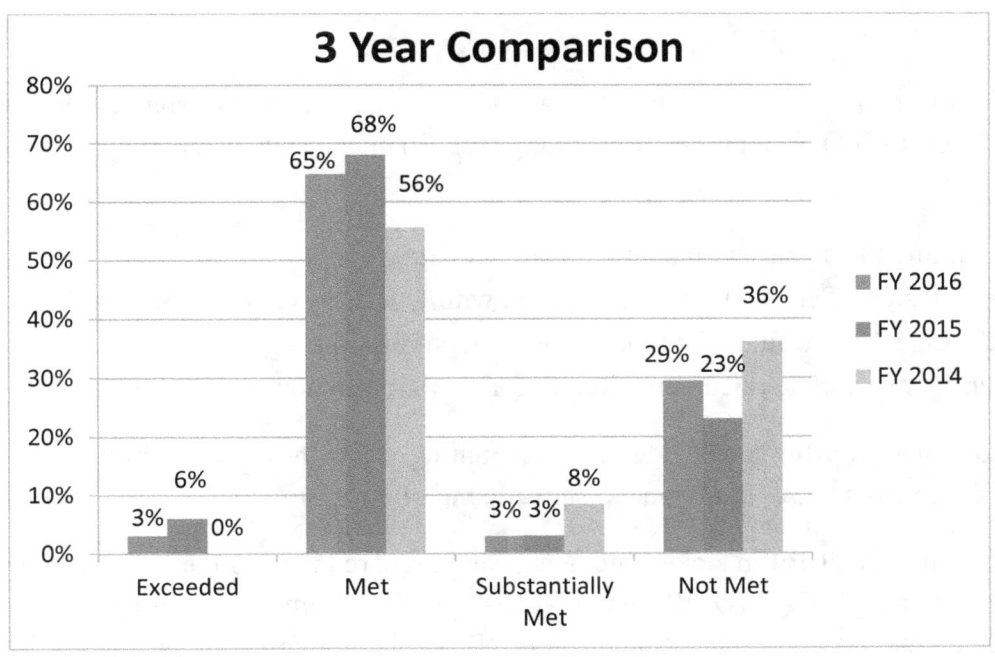

3 Year Comparison

In FY 2016, the Commission has met, substantially met, or exceeded 71 percent of its goals.

D. Federal Managers' Financial Integrity Act (FMFIA)

OMB Circular A-123, Management's Responsibility for Internal Control and the Federal Managers' Financial Integrity Act (FMFIA) require Federal managers to improve accountability and effectiveness of Federal programs and operations by establishing, assessing, correcting, and reporting on internal controls. Commission management is responsible for establishing and maintaining an effective internal control and financial management system. The Commission's Administrative Instruction 1-13 requires office and division heads to complete an annual self-assessment of internal controls as of June 30 each year.

In FY 2016, all offices and division heads completed a self-assessment. The Commission identified one material weakness. The Agency lacks adequate controls to ensure reliability of financial reporting. Regional and headquarters' offices did identify several immaterial weaknesses. Based on this evaluation, the Commission is able to provide a statement of assurance that the internal controls except for internal controls over financial reporting are compliant.

The Commission continues to use the USDA OCFO as its accounting shared services provider. USDA OCFO provides a broad range of financial and accounting services including:

- maintaining the agency's standard general ledger,
- using a system (Pegasys) that is compliant with federal government standards,
- generating required financial reports for the Commission, and
- requiring appropriate documentation of financial transactions prior to payment.

With the Commission's limited budget and accounting staff, the services provided by USDA OCFO are essential to the financial stewardship of our resources.

The Commission's FY 2016 financial statements were prepared in accordance with Office of Management and Budget (OMB) Circular A-136. The Commission prepares four financial statements: Balance Sheet, Statement of Net Costs, Statement of Changes in Net Position, and Statement of Budgetary Resources.

Balance Sheet

The balance sheet presents amounts of future economic benefits owned or managed by the reporting entity (assets), amounts owed by the entity (liabilities), and amounts which comprise the difference (net position).

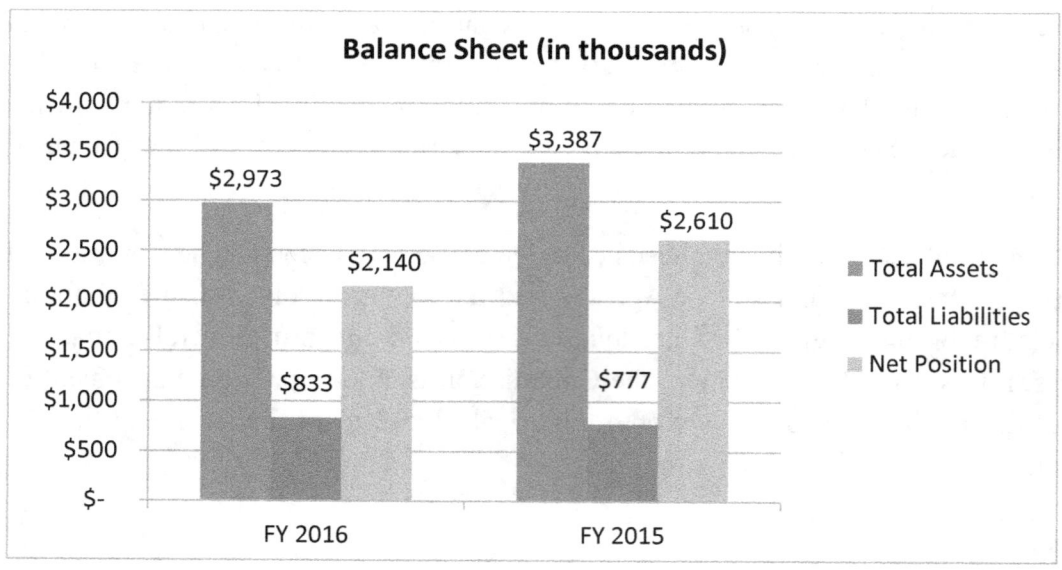

The Commission's total assets decreased from $3,387,430 in FY 2015 to $2,972,702 in FY 2016. The Commission's assets consist mainly of Fund Balance with Treasury (FBWT)

with minimal amounts in General Property, Plant, and Equipment. Total liabilities increased from $777,366 in FY 2015 to $832,891 in FY 2016. Net Position decreased from $2,610,095 in FY 2015 to $2,139,811 in FY 2016.

Statement of Net Costs

The Statement of Net Cost presents the annual cost of operating the Commission's programs.

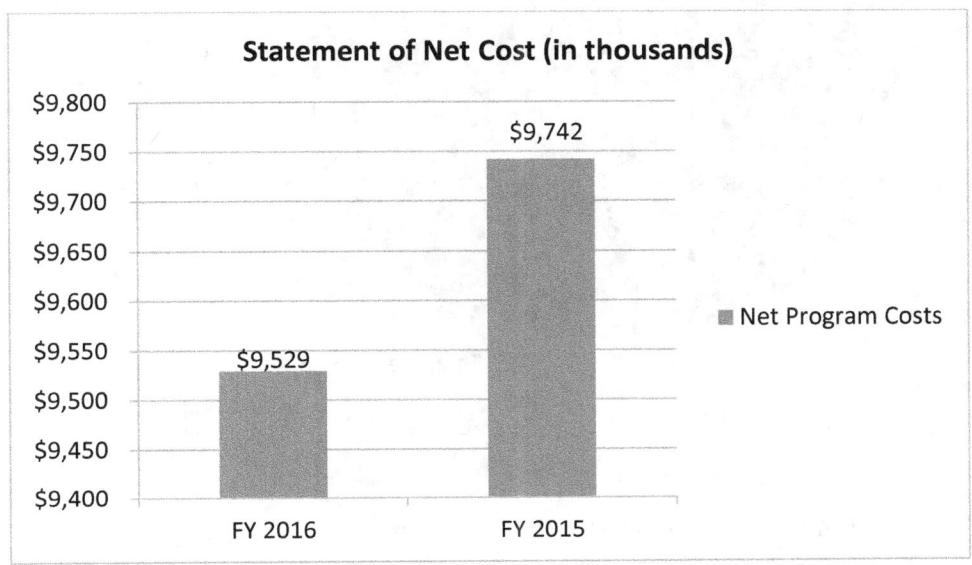

The Commission's net cost of operation decreased from $9,741,850 in FY 2015 to $9,529,414 in FY 2016.

Statement of Budgetary Resources

The Statement of Budgetary Resources provides information on the sources of budgetary resources and their status at the end of the period. The Commission received $9,200,000 in new budgetary authority in FY 2016. The Total Budgetary Resources and Status of Budget Resources increased from $11,611,165 in FY 2014 to $11,730,900 in FY 2016.

Resources by Major Object Class

FY 2015 Obligations by Object Class (in thousands)

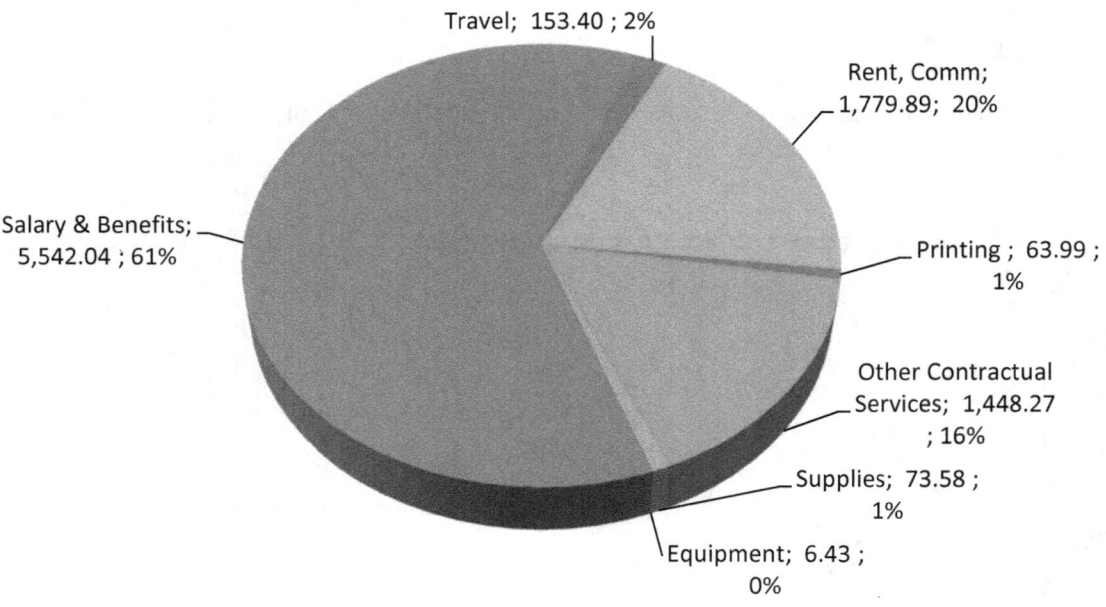

Travel; 153.40 ; 2%

Rent, Comm; 1,779.89; 20%

Salary & Benefits; 5,542.04 ; 61%

Printing ; 63.99 ; 1%

Other Contractual Services; 1,448.27 ; 16%

Supplies; 73.58 ; 1%

Equipment; 6.43 ; 0%

During FY 2016, the Commission obligated $ 9,034,237 of its FY 2016 appropriation of $9,200,000 for an obligation rate of 98.2 percent. Salary and Benefits, Other Contractual Services, and Rent and Communications consume 97 percent of the Commission's obligations. The remaining 3 percent consists of travel, printing, supplies, and equipment.

F. Limitations on Financial Statements

The principal financial statements have been prepared to report the financial position and results of operations of the entity, pursuant to the requirements of 31 U.S.C. 3515 (b). While the statements have been prepared from the books and records of the entity in accordance with GAAP for Federal entities and the formats prescribed by OMB, the statements are in addition to the financial reports used to monitor and control budgetary resources, which are prepared from the same books and records. The statements should be read with the realization that they are for a component of the U.S. Government, a sovereign entity.

G. Management Statement of Assurance

The U.S. Commission on Civil Rights is responsible for establishing and maintaining effective internal control and financial management systems that meet the objectives of the Federal Managers' Financial Integrity Act (FMFIA). The Commission can provide reasonable assurance that its internal controls over financial reporting as of June 30, 2016 except for Undelivered Orders and Recoveries of Prior Years Obligations were operating effectively in the design or operation of the internal control over financial reporting. The Commission identified lack of controls to ensure reliability of Undelivered Orders and Recoveries of Prior Years Obligations as a material weakness.

UNITED STATES COMMISSION ON CIVIL RIGHTS

1331 Pennsylvania Ave, NW • Suite 1150 • Washington, DC 20425 www.usccr.gov

Statements of Assurance: Federal Managers' Financial Integrity Act, OMB Circular A-123, and the Federal Financial Managers Improvement Act of 1996

The management of the U.S. Commission on Civil Rights is responsible for establishing and maintaining effective internal control and financial management systems that meet the objectives of the Federal Managers' Financial Integrity Act (FMFIA). The Commission conducted its assessment of the effectiveness of internal control and efficiency of operations and compliance with applicable laws and regulations in accordance with OMB Circular A-123, Management's Responsibility for Internal Control. Based on the results of this evaluation, the Commission can provide reasonable assurance that our internal control over the effectiveness and efficiency of operations, and compliance with applicable laws and regulations as of September 30, 2016, were operating effectively and no material weaknesses were found in the design or operation of the internal controls.

In addition, the Commission conducted its assessment of the effectiveness of internal control over financial reporting. This includes safeguarding of assets and compliance with applicable laws and regulations. Based on the results of this evaluation, the Commission can provide reasonable assurance that its internal controls over financial reporting as of June 30, 2016 except for Undelivered Orders and Recoveries of Prior Years Obligations were operating effectively in the design or operation of the internal control over financial reporting. The Commission identified lack of controls to ensure reliability of Undelivered Orders and Recoveries of Prior Years Obligations as a material weakness.

The performance and financial data contained in this report, to the best of my knowledge, are complete and reliable.

Mauro Morales
Staff Director
United States Commission on Civil Rights
November 15, 2016

Section II: Performance Report

Our agency performs an important role in identifying emergent civil rights trends and evaluating federal agency civil rights enforcement programs. Our agency's strategic plan articulates the Commission's vision for executing our vital mission from FY 2016 through FY 2018 and for overcoming various administrative challenges. The plan contains six long-term strategic goals. Associated with each of these goals are one or more objectives or specific statements of what we plan to accomplish.

Our FY 2016 annual performance plan includes performance goals and targets that support the accomplishment of our strategic objectives. Below, we describe our FY 2016 annual plan performance targets. We evaluate and report our performance using these categories: Exceeded, Met, Substantially Met, and Not Met.

A. Reliability of Performance Data

Over the course of the year, Commission managers monitor and record their progress on achieving their performance goals.

In headquarters, the Office of General Counsel, Office of Civil Rights Evaluation, and Office of Management typically begin reporting performance data during the last quarter of the fiscal year. The Office of General Counsel and Office of Civil Rights Evaluation performance data is on the quantity, quality, effectiveness, and efficiency of their civil rights reports and briefings. The Office of Management reports on the administrative functions of the Commission. The Staff Director reviews and validates headquarters performance data for accuracy.

For our regional staff, performance management involves submitting end-of-the-year performance data using standardized agency reporting forms, end-of-year reports on their complaint referral services, and participating in periodic meetings with the chief of RPCU.

B. Strategic Goal A: The Commission will function as an effective civil rights watchdog and conduct studies and issue publications on important issues of civil rights.

The below pie chart shows how well we executed the activities, strategies, and initiatives we proposed to achieve in our first strategic goal of functioning as an effective civil rights watchdog and conduct studies and issue publications.

Strategic Goal A: Function as an Effective Civil Right Watchdog and Conduct Studies and Issue Publications on Important Issues of Civil Rights
(actual v. target performance)

Exceeded
100%

This fiscal year we exceeded 100 percent of Strategic Goal A his goal.

Fifty years after the founding of the Commission, an extensive governmental structure has been erected to protect civil rights. Bulwarks against discrimination are well-entrenched features of America's legal landscape and include the Equal Employment Opportunity Commission (EEOC); the Office of Federal Contract Compliance Programs (OFCCP) of the Department of Labor; the Civil Rights Division of the Department of Justice; the Office for Civil Rights of the Department of Education; the Office of Civil Rights of the Department of Health and Human Services; the Office of Fair Housing and Equal Opportunity of the Department of Housing and Urban Development; the various state civil and human rights commissions; the innumerable local civil and human rights commissions; the tens of thousands of private attorneys who pursue actions under Title VII of the Civil Rights Act of 1964, Title VI and Title IX of the 1972 Education Amendments, the Voting Rights Act of 1965, the Fair Housing Act of 1968, the Civil Rights Act of 1991, Executive Order 11246, the Americans with Disabilities Act, the Age Discrimination in Employment Act, and their state and local comparatives; and affirmative action compliance officers in thousands of corporations and political subdivisions.

The Commission's unique position in the civil rights landscape allows it to think and act prospectively. We sought to accomplish this by functioning as an effective Civil Rights watchdog and conducting studies and issuing publications on important issues of Civil Right.

i. Briefings

To promote public awareness of current civil rights laws, remedies, and enforcement agencies, we held four successful briefings.

Public Education Funding Inequality in an Era of Increasing Concentration of Poverty and Resegregation

The purpose of this briefing was to examine the funding of K-12 education and how the inequitable distribution of these funds negatively and disproportionately impact the educational opportunities of low-income and minority students. The briefing also addressed how the practice of underfunding public schools has exacerbated the academic achievement gap in an era where the nation's most vulnerable children are increasingly educated in highly segregated and under-resourced schools.

Quiet Crisis: Federal Funding and Unmet Needs in Indian Country, 2016 Update

The purpose of this briefing was to examine education, health, public safety, housing, rural development and economic opportunity in the Native American Community. The briefing and report will be an update to the Commission's 2003 Report: A Quiet Crisis: Federal Funding and Unmet Needs in Indian Country. Commissioners and Panelists discussed the steps taken to implement the recommendations presented in the 2003 report as well as future actions that must be taken to address unmet needs in Indian country. The Commission heard testimony from Native American Advocacy Groups and Federal and State Government Officials.

Environmental Justice: Toxic Materials, Poor Economies, and the Impact on the Environment of Low-Income, Minority Communities

The Commission briefing for its statutory report examined the Environmental Protection Agency's (EPA) work under Title VI of the Civil Rights Act of 1964 and Order (E.O.) 12,898, with a focus on the civil rights implications of the placement of coal ash disposal facilities near minority and low-income communities. Commissioners and panelists addressed a variety of questions including how to reduce the backlog of Title VI complaints, what more can be done to address the current disproportionate placement of coal ash impoundment sites and landfills in areas with primarily minority and low income residents, and what can be done to prevent such placements in the future. The briefing addressed the first coal ash rule published in spring of 2015, the EPA and other agencies' collaborative work on environmental justice, including that enforced under Title VI.

Municipal Policing and Courts: A Search for Justice or a Quest for Revenue

The purpose of this briefing was to examine how municipalities may target individuals within the criminal justice system to raise revenue via the collection of fees and fines. Municipalities reliant on criminal justice revenue streams may interfere with the judiciary's independent role, divert attention from the courts' essential functions, and adversely impact the most vulnerable residents, principally those living in or near poverty. The briefing examined the national implication of revenue generating tactics in similarly situated jurisdictions across the country and addressed due process issues and the enforcement of other federal laws that violate Title VI of the Civil Rights Act of 1964.

ii. Commission Reports

Increasing Compliance with Section 7 of the National Voter Registration Act.

The report examines state compliance with the National Voter Registration Act's mandate to provide voter registration forms and assistance to those utilizing public assistance and disability agencies, and the efforts of the Department of Justice and private citizens in enforcing the mandate, found in Section 7 of the Act.

The report also looks at trends in voter registration modernization, including electronic and automatic registration, and the use of health benefit exchanges to register voters. The Commission held a briefing on April 19, 2013. From this testimony and subsequent research, a majority of the Commission made a number of findings and recommendations.

Highlights of the findings include:

1. Providing for voter registration at public assistance offices is important to improve minority registration and participation in the election process. U.S. Census Bureau statistics show Hispanics and blacks were, respectively, three and four times more likely than whites to register to vote at a public assistance agency. At least one state has observed that having voter registration offered at public assistance offices benefits voters of all demographics.

2. Providing for voter registration at public assistance offices is vital for citizens with disabilities. These citizens struggle with poverty at twice the rate of citizens without disabilities and thus may be more likely to register to vote at those offices.

3. Providing for voter registration at public assistance offices is also important for Limited English Proficient persons, who are more likely to be living in poverty than English proficient individuals. The Election Assistance Commission has translated the National Mail Voter Registration form into Spanish and eight Asian languages.

4. Congress provided the Department of Justice with authority to sue state agencies that fail to comply with the National Voter Registration Act. The Department has additional tools, including publishing guidance on implementing the National Voter Registration Act, conducting investigations, sending letters of intent to enforce the National Voter Registration Act, and reviewing state data reported to the Election Assistance Commission.

5. A recent Election Assistance Commission Report shows that compliance intervention—including cooperative work and/or lawsuits by the Department of Justice or private litigants resulted in seven of the ten top-performing states under Section 7. Litigation is an effective tool to enforce state compliance with Section 7.

6. Integrating voter registration procedures within existing agency processes, including automatic opt out and online processes, is essential to effective National Voter Registration Act compliance. Integrated computerized processes can improve Section 7 compliance and voter registration rates among low-income citizens, Limited English Proficient citizens, and citizens with disabilities.

7. The most efficient and cost-effective registration process for states to meet the National Voter Registration Act's requirements is to provide an electronic automatic "opt out" registration process. This process clarifies any confusion an applicant may have regarding the necessity to register to vote in order to receive benefits. It eliminates hard-copy error from the process and does not rely on an agency employee's memory to comply with the registration process.

Highlights of the recommendations include:

1. States should have strong oversight of their National Voter Registration Act programs, and Congress should fund a single point of contact in the State Board of Elections who coordinates National Voter Registration Act activities in the state.

2. Because compliance with the National Voter Registration Act requires the management of a large volume of data on both voter registration forms and declination forms, Congress should provide resources for states to learn about and invest in technology that streamlines data processing.

3. Congress should increase resources for the Department of Justice to provide technical assistance, training about and enforcement of the National Voter Registration Act.

4. Congress should expand Section 7 to require federal agencies to agree to be designated as a covered agency under Section 7 when requested by states.

5. The Election Assistance Commission should encourage states to move to electronic voter registration rather than relying solely on paper forms, and integrate registration seamlessly with other electronically covered transactions.

6. The Election Assistance Commission should reexamine whether it should translate the National Mail Voter Registration form into additional languages.

7. The Department of Health and Human Services should ensure federally facilitated Health Benefit Exchanges comply with Section 7. Federal employees who assist the public

must be trained in assisting with voter registration, and training must be offered on an ongoing basis.

The full report can be found at:

http://www.usccr.gov/pubs/NVRA-09-07-16.pdf

Peaceful Coexistence: Reconciling Nondiscrimination Principles with Civil Liberties

The report examined the balance struck by federal courts, foremost among them the U.S. Supreme Court, in adjudicating claims for religious exemptions from otherwise applicable nondiscrimination law.

The Commission heard testimony from experts and scholars in the field and a majority of the Commission made findings and recommendations. Some of those findings were that:

1. Civil rights protections ensuring nondiscrimination, as embodied in the Constitution, laws, and policies, are of preeminent importance in American jurisprudence.

2. Religious exemptions to the protections of civil rights based upon classifications such as race, color, national origin, sex, disability status, sexual orientation, and gender identity, when they are permissible, significantly infringe upon these civil rights.

3. The First Amendment's Establishment Clause constricts the ability of government actors to curtail private citizens' rights to the protections of non-discrimination laws and policies. Although the First Amendment's Free Exercise Clause and the Religious Freedom Restoration Act (RFRA) limit the ability of government actors to impede individuals from practicing their religious beliefs, religious exemptions from nondiscrimination laws and policies must be weighed carefully and defined narrowly on a fact-specific basis.

4. With regard to federal government actions, RFRA protects only First Amendment free exercise rights of religious practitioners and not their Establishment Clause freedoms. Prior to RFRA's enactment, the U.S. Supreme Court had held in Employment Division v. Smith, 494 U.S. 872 (1990), that the First Amendment "had never been held to excuse [an individual's religiously motivated conduct] from compliance with an otherwise valid law prohibiting conduct that the state is free to regulate." This holding strengthened nondiscrimination laws and policies against actors who asserted religious justification for civil rights discrimination. RFRA now supersedes Smith as a controlling source of federal authority. Some states have enacted statutes modeled after RFRA which impact state-level nondiscrimination civil liberties and civil rights protections.

Recommendations included:

1. Overly-broad religious exemptions unduly burden nondiscrimination laws and policies. Federal and state courts, lawmakers, and policy-makers at every level must tailor religious exceptions to civil liberties and civil rights protections as narrowly as applicable law requires.

2. RFRA protects only religious practitioners' First Amendment free exercise rights, and it does not limit others' freedom from government-imposed religious limitations under the Establishment Clause.

3. In the absence of controlling authority to the contrary such as a state-level, RFRA-type statute, the recognition of religious exemptions to nondiscrimination laws and policies should be made pursuant to the holdings of Employment Division v. Smith, which protect religious beliefs rather than conduct.

4. Federal legislation should be considered to clarify that RFRA creates First Amendment Free Exercise Clause rights only for individuals and religious institutions and only to the extent that they do not unduly burden civil liberties and civil rights protections against status-based discrimination.

5. States with RFRA-style laws should amend those statutes to clarify that RFRA creates First Amendment Free Exercise Clause rights only for individuals and religious institutions. States with laws modeled after RFRA must guarantee that those statutes do not unduly burden civil liberties and civil rights with status-based discrimination.

The full report can be found at:

http://www.usccr.gov/pubs/Peaceful-Coexistence-09-07-16.PDF

Environmental Justice: Examining the Environmental Protection Agency's Compliance and Enforcement of Title VI and Executive Order 12,898

This report examines whether the Environmental Protection Agency ("EPA") is complying with its environmental justice obligations. The Commission heard testimony from the EPA, experts and scholars in the field, and a majority of the Commission made findings and recommendations.

Some of the findings are:

1. EPA's definition of environmental justice recognizes environmental justice as a civil right, fair treatment and meaningful involvement of all people regardless of race, color, notional origin, or income with respect to the development, implementation, and enforcement of environmental laws, regulations and policies.

2. Racial minorities and low income communities are disproportionately affected by the siting of waste disposal facilities and often lack political and financial clout to properly bargain with polluters when fighting a decision or seeking redress.

3. The EPA has a history of being unable to meet its regulatory deadlines and experiences extreme delays in responding to Title VI complaints in the area of environmental justice.

4. EPA's Office of Civil Rights has never made a formal finding of discrimination and has never denied or withdrawn financial assistance from a recipient in its entire history, and has no mandate to demand accountability within the EPA.

5. While lacking formal research on links to cancer, it is known that the heavy metals contained in coal ash are known as "hazardous substances" and can potentially damage all major organ systems. Not only do the toxic substances found in coal ash become absorbed up the food chain, but they also contaminate the environment (humans and animals) through spills, dam leaks, and sewage pipe breaks.

6. Whether coal ash facilities are disproportionately located in low-income and minority communities depends on how the comparison is done, but the EPA did find the percentage of minorities and low income individuals living within the catchment area of coal ash disposal facilities is disproportionately high when compared to the national average. The EPA did not fully consider the civil rights impacts in approving movement and storage of coal ash.

7. The EPA's Final Coal Ash Rule negatively impacts low-income and communities of color disproportionately, and places enforcement of the Rule back on the shoulders of the community. This system requires low-income and communities of color to collect complex data, fund litigation and navigate the federal court system - the very communities that the environmental justice principles were designed to protect.

Highlights of the recommendations include:

1. The EPA should not eliminate the deadlines related to processing and investigating Title VI complaints, nor should it adopt a phased-approach to conducting post-award compliance reviews. The EPA should include affected communities in the settlement process.

2. The EPA should bring on additional staff to meet current and future needs, and to clean up its backlog of Title VI complaints. EPA should empower and support the efforts of the Office of Civil Rights (and Deputy Officers), continue sharing expertise among regions, and provide the Office with the necessary tools to hold accountable other EPA entities in minority jurisdictions.

3. Coal Ash should be classified as "special waste" and federal funding should be provided for research on health impact of coal ash exposure to humans. The EPA should provide assistance to affected communities to help enforce the Coal Ash Rule. In addition, the EPA should test drinking water wells, and assess high-risk coal-ash dams and coal ash disposal sites.

4. EPA should provide technical assistance to minority, tribal, and low-income communities to help enforce the Coal Ash Rule and should promulgate financial assurance requirements for coal ash disposal as soon as possible under RCRA or CERCLA authority.

5. EPA should prohibit its state partners, and any recipients of EPA funds, from allowing industrial facilities in their jurisdiction to operate without the appropriate permits and the EPA should enforce permitting requirements and re-evaluate remediation fund reserve guidelines.

The full report can be found at:

http://www.usccr.gov/pubs/Statutory_Enforcement_Report2016.pdf

   C. Strategic Goal B: The Commission will regularly provide new, objective information and analysis on civil rights issues.

We continue to work to provide new, objective information and analysis. The Commission will regularly conduct original fact-finding and/or a novel statistical data review in civil rights investigation. All Commission products will be prepared using standards that provide for maximum objectivity. We seek to accomplish this by:

- Selecting an investigation as part of its annual project planning.
- Strengthening employees' ability to conduct investigations.
- Improving information quality standards and other procedures regarding the process and review of agency products, as well as the implementation of such standards and procedures.

The below pie chart shows how well we executed the activities, strategies, and initiatives we proposed to achieve in our second strategic goal to regularly provide new, objective information and analysis on civil rights issues.

Strategic Goal B: Provide New, Objective information and Analysis on Civil Rights Issues
(actual v. target performance)

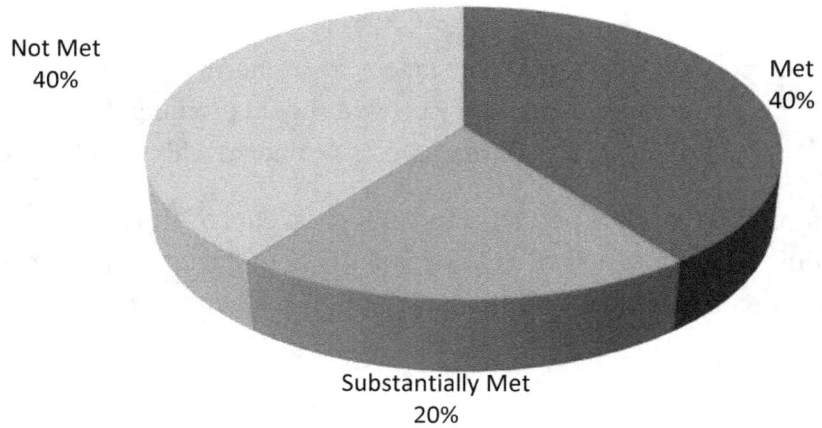

Our statutory report, *Environmental Justice: Examining the Environmental Protection Agency's Compliance and Enforcement of Title VI and Executive Order 12,898* examines whether the Environmental Protection Agency ("EPA") is complying with its environmental justice obligations. The Commission heard testimony from the EPA, experts and scholars in the field, and a majority of the Commission made findings and recommendations. The Commission solicited State Advisory Committees to aid in gathering information at the State and local level. The North Carolina SAC report, *Environmental Justice Issues in North Carolina,* and the Illinois SAC report, *Civil Rights and Environmental Justice in Illinois*, were include in our statutory report.

Appendix B contains additional detail on our performance targets and actual result.

     D. Strategic Goal C: The Commission will cooperate, where appropriate, with other federal agencies to apprise individuals of civil rights laws and policies and to raise public awareness of civil rights.

The Commission will cooperate with other federal agencies to apprise individuals of civil rights laws and policies and raise public awareness of civil rights. The Commission will strengthen its position as a national clearinghouse for civil rights information and consult with the civil rights divisions of other agencies to ensure dissemination of accurate information for the complaint referral process. We seek to accomplish this by:

- Measuring and analyzing web traffic data on the clearinghouse web page to identify top three civil rights areas of interest

- Maintaining up-to-date information on the USCCR complaint referral process.
- Simplifying the telephone complaint referral process

The below pie chart shows how well we executed the activities, strategies, and initiatives we proposed to achieve in our third strategic goal to cooperate with other federal agencies to apprise individuals of civil rights laws and policies and raise public awareness of civil rights.

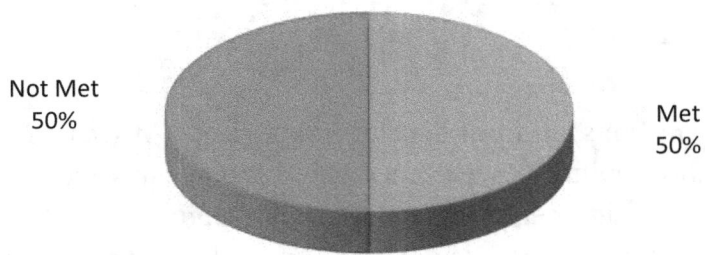

Strategic Goal C: Cooperate with Other Federal Agencies to Apprise Individuals of Civil Rights Laws and Policies and to Raise Public Awareness of Civil Rights Data (actual v. target performance)

Not Met 50%

Met 50%

i.   Clearinghouse Website

The Commission maintains a Clearinghouse Website to serve as a national clearinghouse for information about discrimination or denial of equal protection of the laws because of race, color, religion, sex, age, disability, or national origin.

The Commission provides the public with English and for the first time a Spanish version of Getting Uncle Sam to Enforce Your Civil Rights. This publication is a comprehensive resource for the American public that explains where and how an aggrieved individual can file a discrimination claim.

ii.   Complaint Referral Program

The Commission increases public awareness and federal civil rights enforcement through our complaint referral program. The Office of Civil Rights Evaluation (OCRE) receive complaints alleging denial of civil rights because of color, race, religion, sex, age, disability, or national origin and refers these complaints to the appropriate government agency for investigation and resolution. In FY 2016, the Commission processed 1,595 complaints. OCRE processed 1,595 complaints. Complaints received from regional offices are referred to OCRE for processing. The response time was 10 days or less.

Annual Number of Civil Rights Complaints

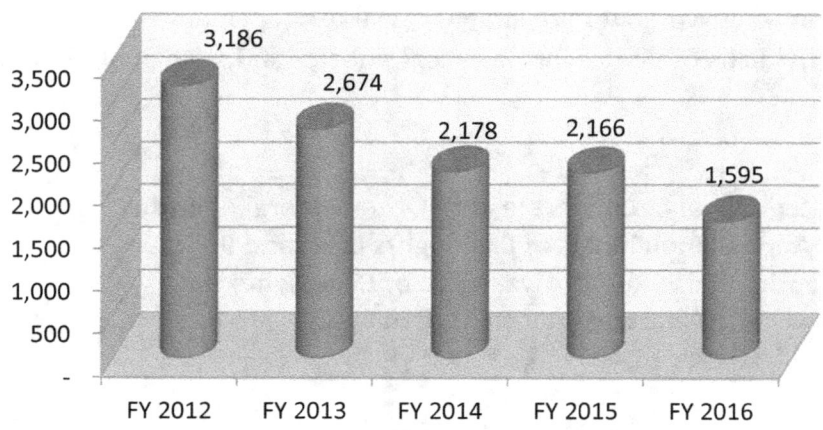

The majority of OCRE complaints are from inmates (30 percent), African Americans (8 percent), and persons with disabilities (4 percent). Of the complaints received, OCRE referred 539 complaints to civil rights enforcement agencies. Approximately 88 percent of referrals went to the Department of Justice (DOJ). Equal Employment Opportunity Commission (EEOC) received 6 percent of referrals while the Department of Health and Human Services (HHS) 5 percent. The remaining referrals went to the Departments of Education, the Housing and Urban Development, and the Department of Transportation.

E. Strategic Goal D: Improve the Commission's profile and effectiveness in communicating with the general public

The Commission will raise public awareness of its work and modernize its information technology to increase access to the Commission's work products. The Commission will improve access to agency publications and expand its complaint process to increase service to persons with disabilities and persons with limited English proficiency. We seek to accomplish this by:

- Expanding press outreach
- Revising and reformatting the website to increase web traffic and access to publications
- Increasing access to Commission briefings and hearings using online tools
- Measuring and analyzing web traffic and written requests for Commission reports.
- Revising and updating the USCCR Website to make electronic and information technology (EIT) accessible to persons with disabilities

- Analyzing complaint line data and written requests for assistance to identify language access needs
- Improving web-based complaint screening process and online guidance to complaints

The below pie chart shows how well we executed the activities, strategies, and initiatives we proposed to achieve in our fourth strategic goal to improve the Commission's profile and effectiveness in communicating with the general public. This fiscal year we met 67 percent of our targets on Strategic Goal D.

Strategic Goal D: Improve the Commission's Profile and Effectiveness in Communicating with the General Public
(actual v. target performance)

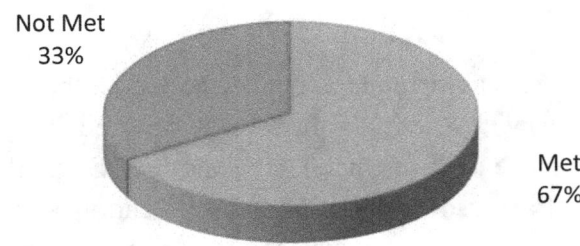

Not Met
33%

Met
67%

To expand our press outreach, the Commission created a press list, issued press releases, participated in speaking engagements, and improved its website.

i.   Press List

The Commission maintains a press list to use to engage the press during any Commission or State Advisory Committee events In addition, the Commission also expanded its press release distribution list to include subject matter and state specific newswires.

ii.   Press Releases

We issued 39 press releases on Commission activities (one press release were also issued in Spanish in an effort to reach Limited English Proficiency Communities), including Commission meetings, SAC activities and reports, and announcements or comments on significant civil rights-related events. This is significant public outreach activity for an agency without full-time, experienced staff in our Public Affairs and Congressional Affairs Units. In addition, our Chairman conducted a press conference on our Statutory Report and participated in multiple press interviews throughout the fiscal year, including as part of the release of the statutory report.

iii. Website Improvements

The Commission FY 2016 – FY 2018 Strategic plan calls for reformatting the Commission's website to increase Google hits. However, due to technical and cost issues, this performance measure is not achievable.

To make reports accessible to persons with disabilities, newly issued Commission reports are available in HTML and text-based versions. As part of the agency's Section 508 plan, users can hear voice playback of the Commissioner's main pages. The Commission is currently working on a web-based complaint screening process and online guidance to improve the complaint process in both English and Spanish

iv. Speaking Engagements.

The Chairman took part in speaking engagements throughout the country this year on the work of the Commission as well as on various projects worked on by the Commission this fiscal year. Some of these events included the National Council of La Raza Annual Convention, the National Bar Association's Annual Convention, and the Arkansas Housing Commission Conference. The Chairman also spoke at numerous other events, such as

- Latino Leaders Luncheon Series Honoring Chairman Martin Castro, Washington, D.C.
- Quinault Indian Nation Listening Session, Washington State
- Speaker Listening Session on Connection between Housing and Violence (IL African American Coalition for Prevention), Chicago, IL
- Keynote Address 2016 IAOHRA Conference" Liberty, Justice and Human Rights for All", Philadelphia, PA
- Keynote Address at the National Civil Rights Conference , Washington DC
- Keynote Speaker Metropolitan Center for Independent Living, Minneapolis, MN
- Meetings with Members of the Wyoming SAC, meetings with Members of the Tribal Councils of the Northern Arapahoe and Eastern Shosoni Tribes, Riverton, WY
- Illinois State Advisory Committee briefing on Environmental Justice, Chicago, IL
- North Carolina State Advisory Committee briefing on Environmental Justice, Greensboro, NC
- Wisconsin State Advisory Committee briefing on Hate Crimes, Milwaukee, WI
- National Congress of American Indians, White House Briefing Preparatory Meeting, Washington, DC

Appendix B contains additional detail on our performance targets and actual result.

F. Strategic Goal E: Continue to strengthen the Commission's financial and operational controls and advance the Commission's mission through management excellence, efficiency, and accountability.

The Commission is committed not only to serving as the nation's conscience on civil rights matters, but also as a model of management excellence, efficiency, and accountability. The Commission is strengthening the Commission's financial, budget, and performance policy, procedures, and reports; improving the strategic management of the Commission's human capital, and refining administrative and clearinghouse services including information technology, acquisition, and library functions.

We seek to accomplish this through our strategic goals by:

- Aligning the Commission's budget submissions with the Agency's strategic plan and annual performance plan
- Ensuring that the Commission's budget submission complies with OMB Circular A-11
- Enhancing financial policy and procedures to ensure reliability of financial reporting
- Monitoring and report on the Commission's progress in achieving its annual performance plan goals and objectives
- Updating and Implementing the Commission's Human Capital Plan to ensure the agency has a highly skilled and flexible workforce to carry out its mission
- Conducting and analyzing Employee Satisfaction surveys and developing specific strategies to address issues
- Conducting training to increase awareness of acquisition processes and procedures
- Complying with Federal Information Security Act (FISMA) requirements
- Leveraging information technology to enhance the productivity and efficiency of the workforce

The below pie chart shows how well we executed the activities, strategies, and initiatives we proposed to achieve in our fifth strategic goal to strengthen the Commission's financial and operational controls and advance the Commission's mission through management excellence, efficiency, and accountability.

**Strategic Goal E: Strengthen the Commission's
Financial and Operational Controls
(actual v. target performance)**

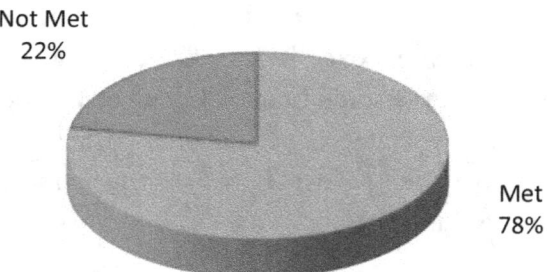

Not Met
22%

Met
78%

Appendix B contains additional detail on our performance targets and actual result.

The Commission budget submission is fully compliant with OMB Circular A-11 and aligned with the Agency's strategic and annual performance plans. The Performance and Accountability report adheres to all relevant guidance. The Agency continues to comply with OMB Cloud Computing Initiatives.

Appendix B contains additional detail on our performance targets and actual result.

G. Strategic Goal F: Increase the participation of our State Advisory Committees (SACs) in the Commission's work.

The Commission has increased and is committed to further increasing the State Advisory Committees' participation in the Commission's work. The Commission is striving to include SAC input in the Commission's program planning process; enhancing collaboration between and among SACs, regional offices, and the Commission; and strengthening the SAC re-chartering process. We seek to accomplish this through our strategic goals by:

- Soliciting SAC involvement in briefings and hearings
- Including regular participation and reports from select SAC chairs as part of the monthly Commission business meetings
- Expanding communication and information sharing via a listserv and use of webinars.
- Achieving and maintaining chartered status for all 51 SACs

We are also pleased that this fiscal year two of our State Advisory Committees conducted briefings in tandem with our statutory enforcement report on environmental justice. The below pie chart shows how well we executed the activities, strategies, and initiatives we proposed to achieve in our sixth strategic goal to increase the participation of our State Advisory Committees (SACs) in the Commission's work.

The Commission has made great strides in increasing the work of our state advisory committees. Our regional staff has been very busy with SAC charters and appointments, reports, fact-finding activities, and complaint referral. We are pleased that this fiscal year we exceeded our performance on this goal, compared to last fiscal year.

i. State Advisory Committee Charters and Appointments

The Commission's state advisory committees operate in compliance with the Federal Advisory Committee Act (FACA). FACA requires that agencies file federal advisory committee charters every two years. In FY 2013, the Commission started filing one charter for all state advisory committees. This allows the Commission to ensure all 51 state advisory committees can operate.

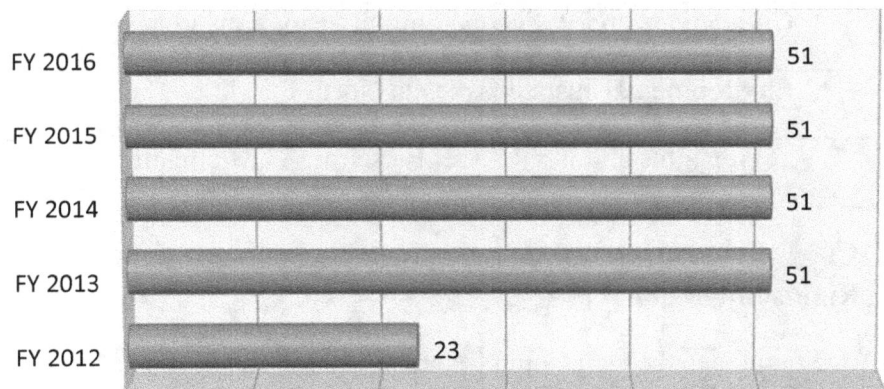

Active State Advisory Committee Charters By Fiscal Year

Fiscal Year	Active Charters
FY 2016	51
FY 2015	51
FY 2014	51
FY 2013	51
FY 2012	23

Along with chartering, commissioners approve recommendations for committee member appointments. Currently 31 state advisory committees have appointed members and 20 state advisory committees are awaiting appointment. Our chartered advisory committee members, working with regional office staff, held 11 civil rights briefings and forums, and 102 planning or business meetings.

In addition to holding meetings, state advisory committees, with regional office support, published the following nine SAC reports in FY 2016:

Advisory Committee	Report Title
Oregon	The Status of Civil Rights in Oregon
Kansas	Seclusion and Restraint of Children With Disabilities in Kansas Schools
Mississippi	Civil Rights and Federal Low Income Childcare Subsidy Distributions in Mississippi
Nebraska	Civil Rights and State-Level Immigration Enforcement in Nebraska
Illinois	Civil Rights and Environmental Justice in Illinois
Oklahoma	Civil Rights and the School to Prison Pipeline in Oklahoma
Missouri	Civil Rights and Police/Community Relations in Missouri
North Carolina	Environmental Justice Issues in North Carolina
Michigan	Civil Rights and Civil Asset Forfeiture in Michigan

The Status of Civil Rights in Oregon

The Oregon Advisory Committee to the U.S. Commission on Civil Rights examined emerging civil rights challenges in four areas: (1) human trafficking, (2) domestic violence, (3) disparities and inequalities in healthcare in Oregon, and (4) the militarization of police forces. As Oregon embarks on the 21st century, the good news regarding the status of civil rights is that the premise that all persons deserve equal rights has widespread general support. Despite overt expressions for equal opportunity, however, centuries of stereotyping and prejudice along racial, religious, ethnic, and gender lines have left lingering scars on society; and cultural and demographic changes continue to present challenges for equal opportunity. The members of the Oregon Advisory Committee approved this report by a vote of 7 yes and 0.

http://www.usccr.gov/pubs/OR_SAC_StatusofCivilRights-WebV.pdf

Seclusion and Restraint of Children with Disabilities in Kansas

On March 23, 2015, the Kansas Advisory Committee to the U.S. Commission on Civil Rights convened a public meeting to examine preliminarily the potential disparate impact of the practice of seclusion and restraint in Kansas schools on children with disabilities. For the purposes of this inquiry, restraint was defined according to the United States Government Accountability Office (GAO) guidelines as "any manual method, physical or mechanic device, material, or equipment that immobilizes or reduces the ability of an individual to move his or her arms, legs, body or head freely." Likewise, seclusion was defined as the "involuntary confinement of an individual alone in a room or area from which the individual is physically prevented from leaving." In this meeting, the Committee sought to begin to understand the extent to which seclusion and restraint practices in both public and private schools may have a disparate, negative impact on students with disabilities. The Committee also sought testimony regarding the potential need for specific federal intervention on this topic. The Committee notes that the focus of this particular inquiry was intentionally limited in scope; including the testimony of four panelists who spoke exclusively on the impact of seclusion and restraint interventions on students with disabilities. The purpose of this inquiry was to determine whether or not sufficient concerns exist to recommend that the Commission consider this topic on a national scale. A majority of the Committee approved this memo and the recommendations included within it.

http://www.usccr.gov/pubs/KS_Advisory_Memo_FINAL.pdf

Civil Rights and Federal Low Income Childcare Subsidy Distributions in Mississippi

On April 29, 2015, the Mississippi Advisory Committee to the U.S. Commission on Civil Rights convened a public meeting via web conference to hear testimony regarding alleged discrimination against recipients of federal low-income childcare subsidies, and the providers who serve them, on the basis of race or color in the State. A second public web conference involving additional testimony followed on May 13, 2015. These hearings were in fulfillment of a project proposal adopted by the Committee on February 27, 2015. Key to the Committee's inquiry was an examination of the federal Child Care and Development Fund (CCDF) and related programs, and the potential for disparate impact on the basis of race or color as a result of the State's discretionary administration of these funds. A majority of the Committee adopted the memo and recommendations included within it.

http://www.usccr.gov/pubs/MississippiCCS_memo_final_with%20appendix.pdf

Civil Rights and State-Level Immigration Enforcement in Nebraska

On May 05, 2015, the Nebraska Advisory Committee to the U.S. Commission on Civil Rights voted to study state level immigration enforcement in Nebraska. Specifically, the Committee sought to examine the civil rights impact of Nebraska's 2009 Legislative Bill 403 (LB 403). Codified in October of 2009 as Nebraska Rev. Stat.§§ 4-108 through 4-114, the law requires

31

that State agencies and their political subdivisions verify the lawful presence of applicants before providing federal, state, or local public benefits. It also requires that State agencies and their political subdivisions verify the work eligibility status of new employees. While the law explicitly states that it "shall be enforced without regard to race, religion, gender, ethnicity, or national origin, "opponents argued that it would necessarily target persons of Hispanic origin in a discriminatory manner. As part of a 2010 public briefing on civil rights concerns in Nebraska, the Committee heard preliminary testimony regarding the potential for such discrimination. In the present study, the Committee sought to examine civil rights concerns that may have surfaced since the initial implementation of LB 403—particularly those related to disparate impact on the basis of race, color, or national origin; and to unequal protection under the law. A majority of the Committee adopted this memo and the recommendations included within it.

http://www.usccr.gov/pubs/MississippiCCS_memo_final_with%20appendix.pdf

Civil Rights and Environmental Justice in Illinois

On March 09, 2016, the Illinois Advisory Committee to the U.S. Commission on Civil Rights convened a public meeting to hear testimony regarding concerns of environmental justice in the State. Key to the Committee's inquiry was an examination of factors contributing to disproportionately poor air quality and other environmental hazards on the basis of race, color, or national origin; particularly in the Chicago neighborhoods of Little Village, South Lawndale, Pilsen, and the City's Southeast side, as well as the City of Waukegan, Illinois. This advisory memorandum results from the testimony provided during the March 09, 2016 meeting of the Illinois Advisory Committee, as well as related testimony submitted to the Committee in writing during the relevant period of public comment. A majority of the Committee adopted this memo and the recommendations included within it. The U.S. Commission on Civil Rights incorporated this memo in Appendix B of its *Environmental Justice: Examining the Environmental Protection Agency's Compliance and Enforcement of Title VI and Executive Order 12,898* report.

http://www.usccr.gov/pubs/Statutory_Enforcement_Report2016.pdf

Civil Rights and the School to Prison Pipeline in Oklahoma

The Oklahoma Advisory Committee to the U.S. Commission on Civil Rights issued this report regarding the civil rights impact of school discipline and juvenile justice policies in the state, which may lead to high rates of juvenile incarceration in what has become known as the "school to prison pipeline." This report details civil rights concerns raised by panelists with respect to school discipline disparities, particularly for students of color, throughout the state of Oklahoma. It discusses the roles of exclusionary school discipline, implicit biases, and poverty in funneling students of color into the school-to-prison pipeline. From these findings, the Committee offers to the Commission recommendations for addressing this problem of national importance.

http://www.usccr.gov/pubs/Oklahoma_SchooltoPrisonPipeline_May2016.pdf

Civil Rights and Police/Community Relations in Missouri

The Missouri Advisory Committee to the U.S. Commission on Civil Rights issued this report regarding the civil rights impact of police and community relations in Missouri, particularly disparities in the use of force on people of color. The contents of this report are primarily based on testimony the Committee heard during hearings on February 23, 2015 in St. Louis, Missouri, and August 20, 2015 in Kansas City, Missouri. This report details civil rights concerns raised by panelists with respect to policing strategies throughout the state of Missouri and discusses the roles of municipal fragmentation, implicit biases, and responses to police misconduct in informing policing strategies and contributing to mistrust between law enforcement and the communities they serve. From these findings, the Committee offers to the Commission recommendations for addressing this problem of national importance.

http://www.usccr.gov/pubs/MOPoliceRelationsReport_Publish.pdf

Environmental Justice Issues in North Carolina

On April 7, 2016, the North Carolina Advisory Committee to the United States Commission on Civil Rights convened a public meeting in the City of Walnut Cove (Stokes County) North Carolina to hear testimony regarding environmental justice issues in the state, particularly issues related to coal ash disposal and its civil rights impacts on communities based upon race and color. The advisory memorandum results from the testimony provided during the April 7, 2016 meeting of the North Carolina Advisory Committee, as well as related testimony submitted to the Committee. The memo is intended to focus specifically on concerns of disparate impact regarding hazardous environmental contamination on the basis of race, color, or other federally protected category. A majority of the Committee adopted this memo and the recommendations included within it. The U.S. Commission on Civil Rights incorporated this memo in Appendix C of its *Environmental Justice: Examining the Environmental Protection Agency's Compliance and Enforcement of Title VI and Executive Order 12,898* report.

http://www.usccr.gov/pubs/Statutory_Enforcement_Report2016.pdf

Civil Rights and Civil Asset Forfeiture in Michigan

The Michigan Advisory Committee to the U.S. Commission on Civil Rights issues this report regarding the civil rights impact of asset forfeiture in Michigan as part of its responsibility to study and report on civil rights issues in the state of Michigan. The contents of this report are primarily based on testimony the Committee heard during public hearings on May 23 and 26, 2016, as well as related testimony submitted to the Committee in writing during the relevant period of public comment. This report is intended to focus specifically on civil rights concerns regarding due process and the potential for disparate impact resulting from asset forfeiture practices in Michigan. A majority of the Committee adopted this memo and the recommendations included within it.

http://www.usccr.gov/pubs/Michigan%20Civil%20Forfeiture%20Report_2016.pdf

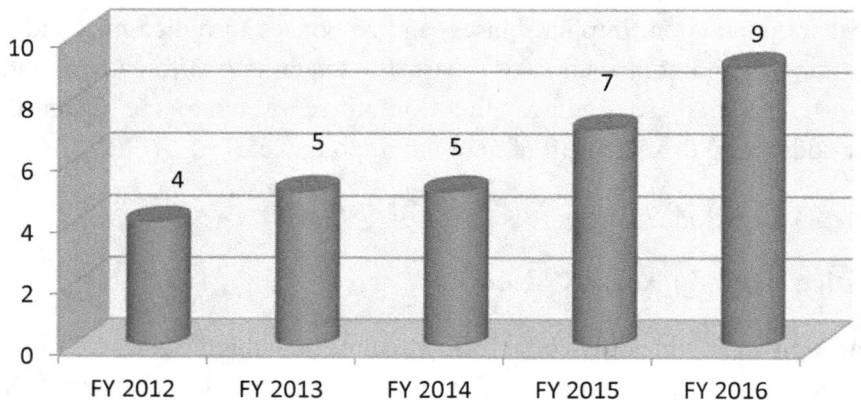

Number of State Advisory Committee Reports by Fiscal Year

iii.   SAC Fact Finding Activity

Regional Office Fact-Finding By Fiscal Year

(meetings, briefings and forums)

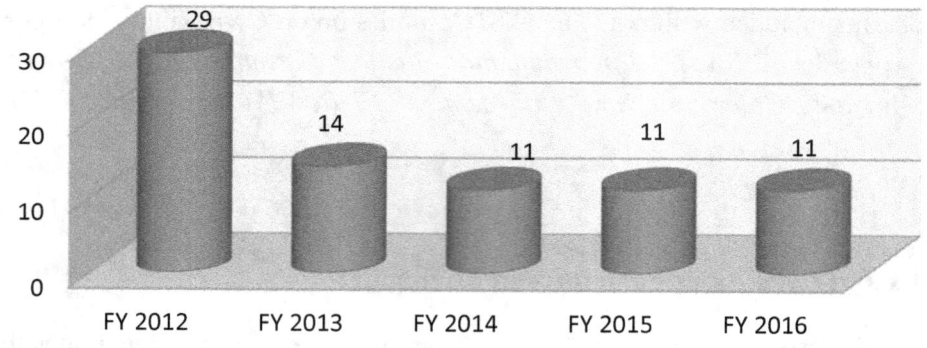

State advisory committees conducted 11 fact-finding activities in FY 2016. All regional offices have the technology to use conference calls and video teleconferencing to conduct public meetings and to provide access to briefings and forums to the public.

Appendix B contains additional detail on our performance targets and actual result.

F. Other Information Related to Annual Performance Reporting

The Government Performance and Results Act of 1993 requires that the Annual Performance Report include information on program evaluations that are relevant to an agency's efforts to attain its goals and objectives as identified in its Strategic Plan or to performance measures and goals reported at the agency level. There were no program evaluations conducted during the fiscal year that meet the criteria established by OMB's Program Assessment Rating Tool (PART) guidance.

No significant contribution to the preparation of our annual performance report was made by a non-federal entity.

Section: III: Auditors Report and Financial Statements

This section demonstrates our commitment to effective stewardship over our funds and compliance with applicable federal financial management laws and regulations. It includes a message from the Chief of Budget and Finance; Financial Statements and Notes to the Financial Statements; Independent Auditors' Report – an independent opinion on the Financial Statements; and Required Supplemental Information.

A. Message from the Chief of Budget and Finance

We received a qualified audit opinion on our fiscal year 2016 financial statements. We have made great progress in improving our internal controls over financial reporting, but we still have more to do.

We will work to resolve the issues that prevented us from receiving an unqualified audit opinion. In FY 2016, we continued our contract with an accounting services provider to supplement our budget staff and provide an accounting system that complies with all applicable federal laws and regulations. We will work with our accounting service provider to improve our internal controls over financial reporting and anticipate an unqualified opinion for FY 2017.

John Ratcliffe
Chief, Budget and Finance Division
November 15, 2016

ALLMOND & COMPANY, LLC   CERTIFIED PUBLIC ACCOUNTANTS

8181 PROFESSIONAL PLACE, SUITE 250
LANDOVER, MARYLAND 20785

Independent Auditors' Report

The Honorable Martin R. Castro
Chairperson
United States Commission on Civil Rights:

Report on the Financial Statements

We have audited the accompanying financial statements of the United States Commission on Civil Rights (the "Commission"), which comprise the balance sheet as of September 30, 2016 and 2015, and the related statement of net cost, changes in net position, and combined statement of budgetary resources for the year ended, and the related notes to the financial statements (hereinafter referred to as the financial statements).

Management's Responsibility for the Financial Statements

Management is responsible for the preparation and fair presentation of these financial statements in accordance with U.S. generally accepted accounting principles; this includes the design, implementation, and maintenance of internal control relevant to the preparation of financial statements that are free from material misstatement, whether due to fraud or error.

Auditors' Responsibility

Our responsibility is to express an opinion on the fiscal year 2016 and 2015 financial statements of the Commission based on our audit. We conducted our audit in accordance with auditing standards generally accepted in the United States of America; the standards applicable to financial audits contained in *Government Auditing Standards* issued by the Comptroller General of the United States; and OMB Bulletin No. 15-02, *Audit Requirements for Federal Financial Statements*. Those standards and OMB Bulletin 15-02 require that we plan and perform the audit to obtain reasonable assurance about whether the financial statements are free of material misstatement.

An audit involves performing procedures to obtain audit evidence about the amounts and disclosures in the financial statements. The procedures selected depend on the auditors' judgment, including the assessment of the risks of material misstatement of the financial statements, whether due to fraud or error. In making those risk assessments, the auditor considers internal control relevant to the entity' s preparation and fair presentation of the financial statements in order to design audit procedures that are appropriate in the circumstances, but not for the purpose of expressing an opinion on the effectiveness of the entity' s internal control. Accordingly, we express no such opinion.

1

An audit also includes evaluating the appropriateness of accounting policies used and the reasonableness of significant accounting estimates made by management, as well as evaluating the overall presentation of the financial statements.

We believe that the audit evidence we have obtained is sufficient and appropriate to provide a basis for our audit opinion.

Basis for Qualified Opinion

Management was unable to provide us with sufficient, competent evidential matter to determine whether all potentially material errors in Undelivered Orders and Recoveries of Prior Years Obligations have been properly corrected in the agency financial system for fiscal years ending 2016 and 2015. Accordingly, a number of amounts could be potentially be misstated on CCR's combined Statement of Budgetary Resources and in the related notes for the years ending September 30, 2016 and 2015 including financial statement captions such as Unobligated Balances – Brought Forward, Recoveries of Prior Years unpaid Obligations, Total Budgetary Resources, Obligations Incurred, Unpaid Obligations brought forward, and Obligated Balance start and end of year.

Qualified Opinion

In our opinion, except for the effects of the matter described in the Basis for Qualified Opinion paragraph, the financial statements referred to above present fairly, in all material respects, the financial position of the U.S. Commission on Civil Rights as of September 30, 2016 and 2015, and its net costs, changes in net position, and budgetary resources for the year then ended in conformity with generally accepted accounting principles in the United States of America.

Emphasis of Matter

As stated in Note 12 to the financial statements, the Commission restated its fiscal year 2015 financial statements in order to correct balances related to accounts payable, accrued payroll and imputed expenses and financing sources which they determined had material errors caused by inadequate internal controls.

Other Information

The information in the *Chairperson's Message, Management and Discussion Analysis* section, and *Other Information* section of this report is not a required part of the basic financial statements, but is supplementary information required by U.S. generally accepted accounting principles. We have applied certain limited procedures, which consisted principally of inquiries of management regarding the methods of measurement and presentation of this information. However we did not audit this information and, accordingly, we express no opinion on it.

2

Other Reporting Required by Government Auditing Standards

Internal Control over Financial Reporting

In planning and performing our audit of the financial statements as of and for the year ended September 30, 2016, we considered the Commission's internal control over financial reporting by obtaining an understanding of the Commission's internal control, determining whether internal controls had been placed in operation, assessing control risk, and performing tests of control to determine auditing procedures for the purpose of expressing our opinion on the financial statements, but not to provide an opinion on the effectiveness of the Commission's internal control over financial reporting. Accordingly, we do not express an opinion on the Commission's internal controls over financial reporting. We limited internal control testing to those necessary to achieve the objectives described in OMB Bulletin No. 15-02. We did not test all internal control relevant to operating objectives as broadly defined by the *Federal Managers' Financial Integrity Act of 1982.*

Our consideration of internal control over financial reporting was for the limited purpose as described in the paragraph above and was not designed to identify all deficiencies in internal control over financial reporting that might be a control deficiency, significant deficiency, or material weakness.

A control deficiency in internal control exists when the design or operation of a control does not allow management or employees, in the normal course of performing their assigned functions, to prevent, or detect and correct misstatements on a timely basis. A significant deficiency is a control deficiency or a combination of control deficiencies, that adversely affects the Commission's ability to initiate, authorize, record, process, or report financial data reliably in accordance with generally accepted accounting principles such that there is more than a remote likelihood that a misstatement of the Commission's financial statements that is more than inconsequential will not be prevented or detected. In our fiscal year 2016 audit, we did not identify any deficiencies in internal control over financial reporting that we considered to be a significant deficiency, as defined above.

However, as described in Exhibit I, we identified certain deficiencies in internal control that we consider to be a material weakness. A material weakness is a significant deficiency, or combination of significant deficiencies, that results in more than a remote likelihood that a material misstatement of the financial statements will not be prevented or detected.

Also, we noted certain additional matters that we have reported to CCR management in a separate letter.

Compliance and Other Matters

As part of obtaining reasonable assurance about whether the Commission's fiscal year 2016 financial statements are free of material misstatements, we performed tests of the Commission's

3

compliance with certain provisions of laws and regulations, with which noncompliance could have a direct and material effect on the determination of the consolidated financial statement amounts, and certain provisions of other laws specified in OMB Bulletin No. 15-02. However, providing an opinion on compliance with those provisions was not an objective of our audit, and accordingly, we do not express such an opinion.

The results of our tests of compliance as described in the preceding paragraph, disclosed an instance of noncompliance or other matters that are required to be reported herein under Government Auditing Standards or OMB Bulletin No. 15-02 and which are described in Exhibit II.

The Commission's Response to Findings

The Commission's responses to the findings identified in our engagement are described immediately following Exhibit II. The Commission's responses were not subjected to the auditing procedures applied in the engagement to audit the financial statements and, accordingly, we express no opinion on the responses.

This report is intended solely for the information of the Commission's management, OMB, and Congress. This report is not intended to be and should not be used by anyone other than these specified parties.

Allmond & Company, LLC

November 15, 2016

4

CONDITION

CCR's internal controls over financial reporting are not sufficiently designed to detect and correct material errors in its financial statements. Based on our review of the financial statements and note disclosures, improvements are needed over reviewing the financial statements and note disclosures for completeness, accuracy, and consistency. Specifically, we noted the following:

- CCR and its service provider did not properly compute and include imputed costs related to Office of Personnel Management (OPM) benefits for years ending September 30, 2016 and 2015 of $254,508 and $244,367 in the financial statements and note disclosures.

- CCR and its service provider incorrectly classified accrued payroll and benefits payable as of September 30, 2016 and 2015 of $246,984 and $155,268 as Accounts Payables.

- CCR did not disclose in their draft financial statement Note 10 a material difference of $3 million between Total Budgetary Resources reported on the FY 2015 SBR and the Budget of the U.S. Government in accordance with OMB Circular A-136.

CCR subsequently corrected all errors noted above.

Also, we noted that management lacks sufficient internal controls over financial reporting to ensure the reliability of its financial reporting. Specifically, we noted that the recorded Undelivered Orders and Recoveries of Prior year Obligations could was not properly supported by sufficient and appropriate documentation.

CRITERIA

Federal Accounting Standards Advisory Board (FASAB), Statement on Federal Financial Accounting Standards (SFFAS) No. 1, *Accounting for Selected Assets and Liabilities*, paragraph 83 and 84, *Other Current Liabilities*, states, "Other current liabilities may include unpaid expenses that are accrued for the fiscal year for which the financial statements are prepared and are expected to be paid within the fiscal year following the reporting date....Typical examples of other current liabilities to be recognized are: (a) accrued employees' wages, bonuses , and salaries for services rendered in the current fiscal year for which paychecks will be issued in the following year."

FASAB SFFAS No. 7, *Accounting for Revenue and Other Financing Sources and Concepts for Reconciling Budgetary and Financial Accounting*, paragraph 73, *Financing Imputed for Cost Subsidies*, states, "Government entities often receive goods and services from other Government

5

41

entities without reimbursing the providing entity for all the related costs. In addition, Government entities often incur cost, such as for pensions that are paid in total or in part by other liabilities. These constitute subsidized costs to be recognized by other accounting standards. An imputed financing source should be recognized equal to the imputed cost. This offsets any effect of imputed cost on net results of operations for the period."

Office of Management and Budget (OMB) Circular A-123, (issued July 2016), Management's Responsibility for Enterprise Risk Management and Internal Controls, Section III, Establishing and Operating an Effective Internal Control System, states the following:

"Management's responsibility is to develop and maintain effective internal control that is consistent with its established risk appetite and risk tolerance levels. In addition, management is responsible for establishing and integrating internal control into its operations in a risk-based and cost beneficial manner, in order to provide reasonable assurance that the entity's internal control operations, reporting, and compliance is operating effectively."

OMB Circular A-136, *Federal Financial Reporting Requirements, (issued October 2016)*, section II.4.9.35, *Note 35 Explanation of Differences between the SBR and the Budget of the US Government*, states the following:

"Agencies should provide a schedule to display the material differences between the SBR and Budget. At a minimum, agencies should display the material differences for comparable line items related to budgetary resources, obligations, distributed offsetting receipts and outlays....Agencies can find comparable information reported in the SBR to the President's Budget in...(b) the "Detailed Budget Estimates by Agency" found in the Appendix for budgetary resources, net outlays and obligations incurred included in the Budget of the United States Government."

Government Accountability Office (GAO), *Standards for Internal Control in the Federal Government* (issued September 2014), *Principle 10 – Design Control Activities, 10.03, Accurate and timely recording of transactions*, states, "Transactions are promptly recorded to maintain their relevance and value to management in controlling operations and making decisions....In addition, management designs control activities so that all transactions are completely and accurately recorded."

The Government Accountability Office (GAO), Standards for Internal Controls in the Federal Government, (issued September 2014), *Principle 10 – Design Control Activities, 10.03, Appropriate documentation of transactions and internal control*, states, "Management clearly documents internal controls and all transactions and other significant events in a manner that allows the documentation to be readily available for examination. The documentation may

6

appear in management directives, administrative policies, or operating manuals, in either paper or electronic form. Documentation and records are properly managed and maintained."

CAUSE

CCR's service provider did not compute OPM imputed costs for fiscal year 2016 and 2015. Also, CCRs internal controls did not detect and correct the error of its service provider.

CCR's service provider incorrectly recorded the payroll accrual adjustment in Accounts Payable. Also, CCRs internal controls did not detect and correct the error of its service provider.

CCR does not have a policy or procedure designed to review the noted disclosures prepared by the service organization to validate the completeness and accuracy of the information presented.

Due to a lack of resources CCR did not forward all the results of the open obligation review performed to its service provider to update the obligated balances recorded in the accounting system.

EFFECT

Gross Costs and Imputed Financing Sources reported on the Statement of Net Costs and Changes in Net Position for FY 2016 and FY 2015 are potentially understated by $254,508 and $244,367 respectively.

The lack of financial reporting internal controls can lead to potential misstatements to the financial statements or line items not being properly classified in accordance with generally accepted accounting principles.

Continuing not to disclose explanations of material differences between the SBR and President's Budget increases the risk of misleading note disclosures and CCR not complying with OMB Circular A-136 financial reporting requirements.

RECOMMENDATION

We recommend that CCR management:

1. Design and implement policies and procedures that document the computation of imputed costs on a quarterly basis. The policy and procedure should also include someone other than the preparer reviewing the computation for completeness and accuracy.

7

2. Design and implement policies and procedure to perform a comprehensive review of the financial statements and note disclosures prepared by the service organization to validate the completeness and accuracy of financial information and verify amounts are presented in accordance with financial reporting requirements.

3. Obtain a detail employee with a background in accounting and federal financial reporting to assists with reviewing the completeness and accuracy of financial information prepared and submitted by the service provider.

8

44

Lack of Compliance with provisions of the Prompt Payment Act

CONDITION

The Prompt Payment Act requires federal agencies to make payments for property or services by the due date specified in the related contract or, if a payment date is not specified in the contract, generally 30 days after the invoice for the amount due are received. If payments are not made within the appropriate timeframe, the agency must pay an interest penalty to the vendor. We noted several instances of noncompliance with this provision of the Prompt Payment Act, where CCR either did not make payments within the specified days or did not pay the correct interest payment.

CRITERIA

U.S. Code Title 31, Subtitle III, Chapter 39 states that under regulations prescribed under section 3903 of this title, the head of an agency acquiring property or service from a business concern, who does not pay the concern for each complete delivered item of property or service by the required payment date, shall pay an interest penalty to the concern on the amount of payment due.

Prompt Payment Act enacted by Congress August 25, 1982:§ 1315.10 Late payment interest penalties, states, "(a) Application and calculation. Agencies will use the following procedures in calculating interest due on late payments: (1) Interest will be calculated from the day after the payment due date through the payment date at the interest rate in effect on the day after the payment due date; (2) Adjustments will be made for errors in calculating interest; (3) For up to one year, interest penalties remaining unpaid at the end of any 30 day period will be added to the principal and subsequent interest penalties will accrue on that amount until paid; (4) When an interest penalty is owed and not paid, interest will accrue on the unpaid amount until paid, except as described in paragraph (a)(5) of this section"

The Government Accountability Office (GAO), Standards for Internal Controls in the Federal Government, section 10.03, *Appropriate documentation of transactions and internal control*, states, "Management clearly documents internal controls and all transactions and other significant events in a manner that allows the documentation to be readily available for examination. The documentation may appear in management directives, administrative policies, or operating manuals, in either paper or electronic form. Documentation and records are properly managed and maintained."

9

CAUSE

The Commission relies on a service provider to make its vendor payments timely however the Commission maintains responsibility for its financial reporting and compliance with laws and regulations. Also, the Commission does not forward its approved vendor invoices to its service provider in a timely manner.

EFFECT

Inadequate monitoring of payments made by its service provider could result in continued noncompliance with the Prompt Payment Act. Not forwarding approved vendor invoices to its service provider could result in continue noncompliance with the Prompt Payment Act.

RECOMMENDATION

We recommend that the Commission management review the payments subjected to the Prompt Payment Act made by its service provider to monitor the timeliness and accuracy of the interest amounts paid to vendors. As well as forward a copy of vendor invoices to its service provider within five business days of approval.

10

UNITED STATES COMMISSION ON CIVIL RIGHTS

1331 Pennsylvania Ave, NW • Suite 1150 • Washington, DC 20425 www.usccr.gov

November 15, 2016

Allmond & Company
8181 Professional Place, Suite 250
Landover, MD 20785

FY 2016 Audit Findings and Recommendations

Attention: Jason Allmond:

We have received and reviewed the independent audit report recently completed by
your firm for the U.S. Commission on Civil Rights ("the Commission"). The
Commission appreciates your effort in conducting an audit of the Commission's
Financial Statements. While your qualified opinion is an improvement over the
qualified disclaimer of opinion we received last year, we are still very concerned. We
are committed to resolving our Undelivered Orders and Recoveries of Prior Year
Obligation internal control deficiencies.

We agree with the following material weaknesses you identified:

- CCR and its service provider did not properly compute and include imputed
  costs related to Office of Personnel Management (OPM) benefits for years
  ending September 30, 2016 and 2015 of $254,508 and $244,367 in the
  financial statements and note disclosures.

- CCR and its service provider incorrectly classified accrued payroll and
  benefits payable as of September 30, 2016 and 2015 of $246,984 and
  $155,268 as Accounts Payables.

- CCR did not disclose in their draft financial statement Note 10 a material
  difference of $3 million between Total Budgetary Resources reported on the
  FY 2015 SBR and the Budget of the U.S. Government in accordance with OMB
  Circular A-136.

- The Prompt Payment Act requires federal agencies to make payments for property or services by the due date specified in the related contract or, if a payment date is not specified in the contract, generally 30 days after the invoice for the amount due are received. If payments are not made within the appropriate timeframe, the agency must pay an interest penalty to the vendor. We noted several instances of noncompliance with this provision of the Prompt Payment Act, where CCR either did not make payments within the specified days or did not pay the correct interest payment.

To help resolve our material weaknesses, we are in the process of hiring an additional staff member.

We are committed to resolving the material weakness you identified in your audit.

Sincerely,

Mauro Morales
Staff Director

UNITED STATES COMMISSION ON CIVIL RIGHTS
BALANCE SHEET
As Of September 30, 2016 and 2015

		2016	Restated 2015
Assets:			
Intragovernmental:	(Note 2)	$ 2,838,419	$ 3,198,395
Fund Balance With Treasury		$ 2,838,419	$ 3,198,395
Total Intragovernmental			
Assets With The Public:			
General Property, Plant and Equipment	(Note 3)	$ 134,284	$ 189,035
Total Assets		$ 2,972,702	$ 3,387,430
Liabilities:	(Note 4)		
Intragovernmental:		$ 5,855	$ 1,238
Accounts Payable		$ 5,855	$ 1,238
Total Intragovernmental			
Liabilities With the Public		$ 219,374	$ 280,286
Accounts Payable			
Other:			
Accrued Funded Payroll and Leave		$ 246,984	$ 155,268
Unfunded Leave		$ 360,679	$ 340,544
Total Liabilities		$ 832,891	$ 777,336
Net Position:			
Unexpended Appropriations - All Other Funds		$ 2,366,206	$ 2,761,603
Cumulative Results of Operations - All Others		$ (226,395)	$ (151,509)
Total Net Position - All Other Funds		$ 2,139,811	$ 2,610,095
Total Net Position		$ 2,139,811	$ 2,610,095
Total Liabilities and Net Position		$ 2,972,702	$ 3,387,430

The accompanying notes are an integral part of these statements.

UNITED STATES COMMISSION ON CIVIL RIGHTS
STATEMENT OF NET COST
As Of September 30, 2016 and 2015

		2016	Restated 2015
Program Costs:			
Gross Cost		$ 9,529,414	$ 9,741,850
Net Program Cost	(Note 5)	$ 9,529,414	$ 9,741,850
Net Cost of Operations		$ 9,529,414	$ 9,741,850

The accompanying notes are an integral part of these statements,

UNITED STATES COMMISSION ON CIVIL RIGHTS

STATEMENT OF BUDGETARY RESOURCES

As Of And For the Years Ended September 30, 2016 and 2015

		2016 Budgetary	2015 Budgetary
BUDGETARY RESOURCES			
Unobligated balance brought forward, October 1		$ 1,825,597	$ 1,954,606
Adjustment of unobligated balance brought forward, October 1 (+ or -)			
Unobligated balance brought forward, October 1, adjusted		$ 1,825,597	$ 1,954,606
Recoveries of prior year unpaid obligations (unobligated balances)		$ 1,098,467	$ 731,870
Other changes in unobligated balance		$ (395,058)	$ (275,316)
Unobligated balance from prior year budget authority, net		$ 2,529,005	$ 2,411,160
Appropriations (discretionary and mandatory)		$ 9,200,000	$ 9,200,000
Spending authority from offsetting collections		$ 1,895	$ 5
Total budgetary resources		$ 11,730,900	$ 11,611,165
STATUS OF BUDGETARY RESOURCES			
New obligations and upward adjustments	(Note 6)	$ 10,014,236	$ 9,836,572
Apportioned		$ 165,763	$ 129,676
Unapportioned		$ 1,550,901	$ 1,644,917
Unobligated balance brought forward, end of year		$ 1,716,664	$ 1,774,593
Total budgetary resources		$ 11,730,900	$ 11,611,165
CHANGES IN OBLIGATED BALANCE			
Unpaid obligations, brought forward, October 1 (gross)		$ 1,372,798	$ 2,155,844
New obligations and upward adjustments		$ 10,014,236	$ 9,836,572
Outlays (gross) (-)		$ (9,166,813)	$ (9,836,743)
Recoveries of prior year unpaid obligations (-)		$ (1,098,467)	$ (731,870)
Unpaid obligations, end of year	(Note 7)	$ 1,121,755	$ 1,423,802
Obligated balance, start of year (net)		$ 1,372,798	$ 2,155,844
Obligated balance, end of year (net)		$ 1,121,755	$ 1,423,802
BUDGET AUTHORITY AND OUTLAYS, NET			
Budget authority, gross (discretionary and mandatory)		$ 9,201,895	$ 9,200,005
Actual offsetting collections (discretionary and mandatory) (-)		$ (1,895)	$ (5)
Budget authority, net (discretionary and mandatory)		$ 9,200,000	$ 9,200,000
Outlays, gross (discretionary and mandatory)		$ 9,166,813	$ 9,836,743
Actual offsetting collections (discretionary and mandatory) (-)		$ (1,895)	$ (5)
Outlays, net (discretionary and mandatory)		$ 9,164,918	$ 9,836,738
Agency outlays, net (discretionary and mandatory)		$ 9,164,918	$ 9,836,738

The accompanying notes are an integral part of these statements.

UNITED STATES COMMISSION ON CIVIL RIGHTS
STATEMENT OF CHANGES IN NET POSITION
As Of And For the Years Ended September 30, 2016 and 2015

	Funds From Dedicated Collections (Consolidated Totals)	All Other Funds (Consolidated Totals)	Eliminations	Consolidated Totals
FY 2016 Current Year				
Cumulative Results of Operations:				
Beginning Balances		$ (151,509)		$ (151,509)
Beginning balance, as adjusted		$ (151,509)		$ (151,509)
Budgetary Financing Sources:				
Appropriations used		$ 9,200,019		$ 9,200,019
Other Financing Sources (Non-Exchange):				
Imputed Financing Sources (Note 8)		$ 254,508		$ 254,508
Total Financing Sources		$ 9,454,527		$ 9,454,527
Net Cost of Operations		$ 9,529,414		$ 9,529,414
Net Change		$ (74,887)		$ (74,887)
Cumulative Results of Operations		$ (226,395)		$ (226,395)
				$ -
Unexpended Apropriations:				
Beginning Balances		$ 2,761,283		$ 2,761,283
Beginning balance, as adjusted		$ 2,761,283		$ 2,761,283
				$ -
Budgetary Financing Sources:				$ -
Appropriations received		$ 9,200,000		$ 9,200,000
Appropriations transferred-in/out				
Other adjustments		$ (395,058)		$ (395,058)
Appropriations used		$ (9,200,019)		$ (9,200,019)
Total Budgetary Financing Sources		$ (395,077)		$ (395,077)
Total Unexpended Appropropriations		$ 2,366,206		$ 2,366,206
Net Position		$ 2,139,811		$ 2,139,811

The accompanying notes are an integral part of these statements,

UNITED STATES COMMISSION ON CIVIL RIGHTS

STATEMENT OF CHANGES IN NET POSITION

As Of And For the Years Ended September 30, 2016 and 2015

	Funds From Dedicated Collections (Consolidated Totals)	All Other Funds (Consolidated Totals)	Eliminations	Consolidated Totals
		FY 2015 Prior Year (Restated)		
Cumulative Results of Operations:				
Beginning Balances		$ (72,285)		$ (72,285)
Beginning balance, as adjusted		$ (72,285)		$ (72,285)
				$ -
Budgetary Financing Sources:				$ -
Appropriations used		$ 9,418,258		$ 9,418,258
				$ -
Other Financing Sources (Non-Exchange):				$ -
Imputed Financing Sources (Note 8)		$ 244,368		$ 244,368
Total Financing Sources		$ 9,662,626		$ 9,662,626
Net Cost of Operations		$ 9,741,850		$ 9,741,850
Net Change		$ (79,224)		$ (79,224)
				$ -
Cumulative Results of Operations		$ (151,509)		$ (151,509)
				$ -
Unexpended Apropriations:				$ -
Beginning Balances		$ 3,255,178		$ 3,255,178
Beginning balance, as adjusted		$ 3,255,178		$ 3,255,178
				$ -
Budgetary Financing Sources:				$ -
Appropriations received		$ 9,200,000		$ 9,200,000
Other adjustments		$ (275,316)		$ (275,316)
Approprations used		$ (9,418,258)		$ (9,418,258)
Total Budgetary Financing Sources		$ (493,575)		$ (493,575)
Total Unexpended Appropropriations		$ 2,761,603		$ 2,761,603
Net Position		$ 2,610,095		$ 2,610,095

The accompanying notes are an integral part of these statements.

U.S. COMMISSION ON CIVIL RIGHTS

GENERAL FUND

NOTE 1   SUMMARY OF SIGNIFICANT ACCOUNTING POLICIES

Reporting entity

The statutory mandate of the U.S. Commission on Civil Rights (the Commission or Agency) is to:

- investigate allegations in writing under oath or affirmation relating to deprivations because of color, race, religion, sex, age, disability, or national origin; or as a result of any pattern or practice of fraud; or of the right of citizens of the United States to vote and have votes counted, 42 U.S.C. §1975a(1); and

- study and collect information, appraise the laws and policies of the federal government, serve as a national clearinghouse for information, and prepare public service announcements and advertising campaigns to discourage discrimination or denials of equal protection of the laws under the Constitution of the United States because of color, race, religion, sex, age, disability, or national origin, or in the administration of justice. 42 U.S.C. §1975a (2).

The Commission also issues a report annually to the President and Congress on monitoring federal civil rights enforcement and establishing state advisory committees in each of the fifty states and the District of Columbia.

Powers

In furtherance of its fact-finding duties, the Commission may hold hearings and issue subpoenas (within states in which hearings are being held and within a 100-mile radius of such sites) for the production of documents and the attendance of witnesses. The Commission also uses depositions and written interrogatories to collect information and testimony about matters subject to hearings or reports. In addition to these more formal measures, the Commission conducts public briefings on existing and emerging civil rights issues and produces briefings reports. The Commission maintains state advisory committees, and consults with representatives of federal, state and local governments, in addition to private organizations.

Since the Commission lacks enforcement powers that would enable it to apply specific remedies in individual cases, its civil rights reports contain findings and recommendations for corrective action by federal and state agencies, and other civil rights stakeholders as deemed appropriate. The Commission also provides a complaint referral service that receives complaints from citizens and other sources and refers them to the appropriate federal, state, or local government agency or private organization for action.

NOTE 1   SUMMARY OF SIGNIFICANT ACCOUNTING POLICIES (Continued)

Organization and structure of the Commission

The Office of the Staff Director is responsible for the day-to-day management of the Commission and for executing the policy direction established by the agency's eight appointed commissioners.

The Commission is comprised of two programmatic units, the Office of General Counsel and the Office of Civil Rights Evaluation and six regional offices. The activities of these regional offices are coordinated through the Regional Programs Coordination Unit. The chief of this unit reports directly to the staff director.

Administratively, the Office Management oversees the work of three divisions: Administrative Services and Clearinghouse (ASCD), Budget and Finance, and Human Resources. Included within ASCD are the Commission's procurement services, public civil rights library, copy/print shop, and information technology services.

Other Commission offices, which at present remain unstaffed, include:
- Congressional Affairs Unit, and
- Equal Employment Opportunity Programs

A summary of significant accounting policies utilized in the preparation of the financial statements is as follows:

Basis of presentation

The Commission's financial statements are prepared from the accounting records of the Commission in accordance with accounting principles generally accepted in the United States (GAAP), and the form and content for entity's financial statements specified by the Office of Management and Budget (OMB) in OMB Circular No. A-136, *Financial Reporting Requirements*, as revised. GAAP for Federal entities are standards prescribed by the Federal Accounting Standards Advisory Board (FASAB), which has been designated the official accounting standards-setting body for the federal government by the American Institute of Certified Public Accountants (AICPA).

NOTE 1   SUMMARY OF SIGNIFICANT ACCOUNTING POLICIES (Continued)

Basis of presentation (continued)

OMB Circular No. A-136 requires agencies to prepare basic statements, which include a balance sheet, statement of net cost, statement of changes in net position and a statement of budgetary resources. The balance sheets present, as of September 30, 2016 and 2015, amounts of future economic benefits owned or managed by the Commission (assets), amounts owed by the Commission (liabilities), and amounts which comprise the difference (net position). The statements of net cost report the full cost of the program, both direct and indirect costs of the output, and the costs of identifiable supporting services provided by other segments within the Commission. The statement of budgetary resources reports the Commission's budgetary activity.

Basis of accounting

The Commission prepares financial statements to report its financial position and results of operations pursuant to the requirements of 31 U.S.C. 3515(b), the Chief Financial Officers Act of 1990 (P. L. 101-576), as amended by the Government Management Reform Act of 1994, and presented in accordance with the requirements in OMB Circular No. A-136, as revised. These statements have been prepared from the Commission's financial records using an accrual basis in conformity with GAAP. The generally accepted accounting principles (GAAP) for federal entities are the standards prescribed by the Federal Accounting Standards Advisory Board (FASAB) and recognized by the AICPA as Federal GAAP. These statements are, therefore, different from financial reports prepared pursuant to other OMB directives that are primarily used to monitor and control the Commission's use of budgetary resources.

Transactions are recorded on an accrual and budgetary basis of accounting. Under the accrual basis of accounting, revenues are recognized when earned, and expenses are recognized when resources are consumed, without regard to the payment of cash. Budgetary accounting principles, on the other hand, are designed to recognize the obligation of funds according to legal requirements, which in many cases is prior to the occurrence of an accrual based transaction. The recognition of budgetary accounting transactions is essential for compliance with legal constraints and controls over the use of federal funds. The Commission uses the cash basis of accounting for some programs with an accrual adjustment made by recording year-end estimates of unpaid liabilities.

Use of estimates

The preparation of financial statements in conformity with GAAP in the United States requires management to make estimates and assumptions that affect the reported amounts of assets and liabilities, and disclosure of contingent assets and liabilities, at the date of the financial statements and the reported amounts of revenue and expenses during the reporting period. Actual results could differ from those estimates.

NOTE 1   SUMMARY OF SIGNIFICANT ACCOUNTING POLICIES (Continued)

Fund balance with Treasury

The Commission maintains its available funds with the Department of the Treasury (Treasury). The fund balance with Treasury is available to pay current liabilities and finance authorized purchases. Cash receipts and disbursements are processed by Treasury and are reconciled with those of Treasury on a regular basis. Note 2, Fund Balance with Treasury, provides additional information.

General property and equipment

General property and equipment (PP&E) consists of equipment used for general operations and internal use software. The basis for recording purchased PP&E is full cost, which includes all costs incurred to bring the PP&E to a form and location suitable for its intended use. The cost of PP&E acquired through donation is the estimated fair market value when acquired. All PP&E with an initial acquisition cost of $5,000 or more and an estimated useful life of two years or more are capitalized, except for internal use software discussed below.

The PP&E is depreciated using the straight-line method over the estimated useful life of the asset. Normal maintenance and repair costs are expensed as incurred. Statement of Federal Financial Accounting Standards (SFFAS) No. 10, *Accounting for Internal Use Software*, requires that the capitalization of internally-developed, contractor-developed and commercial off-the-shelf (COTS) software begin in the software development phase.

For amortization purposes, the estimated useful life for internal use software was determined to be five years. SFFAS No. 10 also requires that amortization begin when the asset is placed in use. Costs below the threshold levels are expensed. Software is depreciated for a period of time consistent with the estimated useful life used for planning and acquisition purposes.

Liabilities

Liabilities are recognized for amounts of probable and measurable future outflows or other sacrifices of resources as a result of past transactions or events. Since the Commission is a component of the U.S. Government, a sovereign entity, its liabilities cannot be liquidated without legislation that provides resources to do so. Payments of all liabilities other than contracts can be abrogated by the sovereign entity. In accordance with public law and existing federal accounting standards, no liability is recognized for future payments to be made on behalf of current workers contributing to the Medicare Health Insurance Trust Fund, since liabilities are only those items that are present obligations of the government. The Commission's liabilities are classified as covered by budgetary resources or not covered by budgetary resources.

NOTE 1   SUMMARY OF SIGNIFICANT ACCOUNTING POLICIES (Continued)

Liabilities Covered by Budgetary Resources are Liabilities incurred which are covered by realized budgetary resources as of the Balance Sheet date. Budgetary resources encompass not only new budget authority but also other resources available to cover liabilities for specified purposes in a given year. Available budgetary resources include: (1) new budget authority, (2) unobligated balances of budgetary resources at the beginning of the year or net transfers of prior year balances during the year, (3) spending authority from offsetting collections (credited to an appropriation or fund account), and (4) recoveries of unexpired budget authority through downward adjustments of prior year obligations. Liabilities are considered covered by budgetary resources if they are to be funded by permanent indefinite appropriations, which have been enacted and signed into law and are available for use as of the Balance Sheet date, provided that the resources may be apportioned by OMB without further action by the Congress and without a contingency having to be met first.

Liabilities Not Covered by Budgetary Resources are liabilities, which are not considered to be covered by budgetary resources. Liabilities Not Covered by Budgetary Resources are combined with liabilities covered by budgetary resources with liabilities on the face of the Balance Sheet.

Accounts payable

Accounts payable primarily consists of amounts due for goods and services received, progress in contract performance, interest due on accounts payable, and other miscellaneous payables.

Accrued payroll and benefits

Accrued payroll and benefits consist of salaries, wages, leave and benefits earned by employees, but not disbursed as of September 30. Liability for annual and other vested compensatory leave is accrued when earned and reduced when taken. At the end of each fiscal year, the balance in the accrued annual leave liability account is adjusted to reflect current pay rates. Annual leave earned but not taken is considered an unfunded liability since this leave will be funded from future appropriations when it is actually taken by employees. Sick leave and other types of leave are not accrued and are expensed when taken.

NOTE 1   SUMMARY OF SIGNIFICANT ACCOUNTING POLICIES (Continued)

Revenue and financing sources

The Commission receives the funding needed to support its programs through an annual Congressional appropriation. The United States Constitution prescribes that no money may be expended by a federal agency unless and until funds have been made available by Congressional appropriation. Appropriations are recognized as financing sources when related expenses are incurred or assets are purchased.

The Commission receives an annual appropriation that may be used within statutory limits. For example, funds for general operations are generally made available for one fiscal year. The Statement of Budgetary Resources presents information about the resources appropriated to the Commission.

Federal employee benefits

Most Commission employees participate in either the Civil Service Retirement System (CSRS) – a defined benefit plan, or the Federal Employees Retirement System (FERS) – a defined benefit and contribution plan. For employees covered under CSRS the Commission contributes a fixed percentage of pay. Most employees hired after December 31, 1983, are automatically covered by FERS. For employees covered under FERS the Commission contributes the employer's matching share for Social Security and Medicare Insurance. A primary feature of FERS is that it offers a Thrift Savings Plan (TSP) into which the Commission automatically contributes one percent of employee pay and matches employee contributions up to an additional four percent of pay.

The U.S. Office of Personnel Management is the administering agency for both of these benefit plans and, thus, reports CSRS or FERS assets, accumulated plan benefits, or unfunded liabilities applicable to federal employees. Therefore, the Commission does not recognize any liability on its balance sheet for pensions, other retirement benefits, and other post employment benefits.

NOTE 2   FUND BALANCE WITH TREASURY

The fund balance with the Treasury is as follows at September 30:

	2016	2015
A. Fund Balance with Treasury		
Appropriated Fund	$ 2,838,419	$ 3,198,395
B. Status of Fund Balance with Treasury		
1) Unobligated Balance		
a) Available	165,763	129,676
b) Unavailable	1,550,902	1,695,921
2) Obligated Balance not yet Disbursed	1,121,754	1,372,798
Total	$ 2,838,419	$ 3,198,395

In fiscal year 2016, the Commission cancelled its fiscal 2011 remaining funds and returned the balance of $395,058.20 to the Treasury.

NOTE 3   GENERAL PROPERTY, PLANT AND EQUIPMENT

Property and equipment consisted of the following at September 30:

	2016	2015
Equipment	$293,070	$293,070
Software	7,684	7,684
	$300,754	$300,754
Less: Accumulated depreciation		
Equipment	161,454	108,244
Software	5,016	3,476
	$166,470	$111,720
Property and Equipment Net	$134,284	$189,034

Depreciation and amortization expense for the fiscal years ended September 30, 2016 and 2015 was $54,751 and $58,349, respectively.

NOTE 4 LIABILITIES NOT COVERED BY BUDGETARY RESOURCES

The Commission's total liabilities were comprised of the following at September 30:

	2016	2015
Liabilites not covered by budgetary resources with the public		
Other (unfunded leave liability)	360,679	340,544
Liabilities covered by budgetary resources	472,212	436,792
Total Liabilities	$ 832,891	$ 777,336

Liabilities not covered by budgetary resources included liabilities for which congressional action is needed before budgetary resources can be provided. Although future appropriations to fund these liabilities are likely, it is not certain that appropriations will be enacted to fund these liabilities.

Liabilities covered by budgetary resources as of September 30, 2016 and 2015, were respectively comprised of accounts payable of $472,212 and $436,792.

NOTE 5 INTRAGOVERNMENTAL COSTS

Intra-governmental costs arise from purchases of goods or services from other components of the Federal Government. In contrast, public costs are those that arise from the purchase of goods or services from nonfederal entities. The Commission does not provide services to another federal entity. Intragovernmental costs were comprised of the following for the fiscal years ended September 30:

	Total 2016	Total 2015
Intragovernmental costs	3,192,948	3,034,223
Public costs	6,336,467	6,707,627
Total costs	$ 9,529,415	$ 9,741,850

NOTE 6   APPORTIONMENT CATEGORIES OF OBLIGATIONS INCURRED

Obligations of the Commission represent direct new obligations and upward adjustments against amounts apportioned under category A on the latest Apportionment and Reapportionment Schedule.

	Total 2016	Total 2015
Category A	$ 10,014,236	$ 9,836,572

NOTE 7   UNDELIVERED ORDERS AT THE END OF THE PERIOD

Undelivered orders for the fiscal years ended September 30, 2016 and 2015 amounted to $649,542.13 and $960,697, respectively.

NOTE 8   IMPUTED FINANCING SOURCES

The Commission recognizes as imputed financing, the costs of future benefits, which include health benefits, life insurance, pension, and post-retirement benefit expenses for current employees. The assets and liabilities associated with such benefits are the responsibility of the administering agency, OPM. For the fiscal years ended September 30, 2016 and 2015, imputed financing was as follows:

	Total 2016	Total 2015
Office of Personnel Management	254,508	244,638
Total costs	254,508	244,638

NOTE 9   OPERATING LEASES

The Commission has various leases for offices and branches throughout the United States. The longest of those obligations extends through 2025. Certain of the leases contain renewal options and escalation clauses. No leases include restrictions on the Commission's activities. The aggregate rent expense totaled $1,490,464 and $1,467,329 for fiscal years ended September 30, 2016 and 2015, respectively. Future minimum rent payments for the fiscal years ended September 30, are as follows:

	2016
2017	1,490,507
2018	1,443,622
2019	1,401,687
2020	1,354,024
2021	1,328,185
Thereafter	1,013,171
Total	$ 8,031,196

NOTE 10 BUDGETARY RESOURCE COMPARISONS TO THE BUDGET OF THE UNITED STATES GOVERNMENT

The President's Budget that will include fiscal year 2016 actual budgetary execution information has not yet been published. The President's Budget is scheduled for publication in February 2017 and can be found at the OMB Web site http://www.whitehouse.gov/omb/.

Material differences exist between the amounts reported in the fiscal year 2015 Statement of Budgetary Resources and the 2015 actual amounts reported in the 2016 Budget of the United States Government. The following table identifies the specific differences:

(Millions)	Budgetary Resources	Obligations Incurred	Distributed Offsetting Receipts	Net Outlays
Combined Statement of Budgetary Resources	$ 12	$ 10		$ 10
Expired Unobligated Balances	$ (3)	$ -		$ -
Budget of the U.S. Government	$ 9	$ 10		$ 10

The difference is caused by Expired Unobligated Balances being reported in the Statement of Budgetary Resources but not in the Budget of the United States Government.

NOTE 11 – RECONCILIATION OF NET COST OF OPERATIONS (PROPRIETARY) TO BUDGET

Budgetary resources obligated are obligations for personnel, goods, services, benefits, etc. made by the Commission in order to conduct operations or acquire assets. Other (i.e., non-budgetary) financing resources are also utilized by the Commission in its program (proprietary) operations. For example, spending authority from offsetting collections and recoveries are financial resources from the recoveries of prior year obligations (e.g., the completion of a contract where not all the funds were used) and refunds or other collections (i.e., funds used to conduct operations that were previously budgeted). An imputed financing source is recognized for future federal employee benefits costs incurred for the Commission employees that will be funded by OPM. Changes in budgetary resources obligated for goods, services, and benefits ordered but not yet provided represents the difference between the beginning and ending balances of undelivered orders (i.e., good and services received during the year based on obligations incurred the prior year represent a cost of operations not funded from budgetary resources). Resources that finance the acquisition of assets are budgetary resources used to finance assets and not cost of operations (e.g., increases in accounts receivables or capitalized assets). Financing sources yet to be provided represents financing that will be provided in future periods for future costs that are recognized in determining the net cost of operations for the present period. Finally, components not requiring or generating resources are costs included in the net cost of operations that do not require resources (e.g., depreciation and amortized expenses of assets previously capitalized).

A reconciliation between budgetary resources obligated and net cost of operations (i.e., providing an explanation between budgetary and financial (proprietary) accounting) is as follows (note: in prior years, this information was presented as a separate financial statement, the Statement of Financing):

		FY 2016		FY 2015 (Restated)
Budgetary Resources Obligated	$	10,014,236	$	9,836,572
Spending Authority from Recoveries and Offsetting Collections	$	(1,100,362)	$	(731,865)
Changes in Budgetary Resources Obligated for Goods, Services, and Benefits Ordered but Not Yet Provided	$	286,144	$	313,551
Resources that Finance the Acquisition of Assets	$	-	$	3,357
Imputed Financing from Costs Absorbed by Others	$	254,508	$	244,368
Financing Sources Yet to be Provided	$	20,135	$	17,518
Components Not Requiring or Generating Resources	$	54,751	$	58,349
Net Cost of Operations	$	9,529,414	$	9,741,850

NOTE 12 – RESTATEMENT

In accordance with SFFAS No. 21 Reporting Corrections, Errors, and Changes in Accounting Principles, the Commission restated the FY 2015 financial statements.

The Commission has determined that material errors were caused by inadequate internal control associated with the related processes. Specifically, accounts payable, accrued payroll, and imputed expenses and financing sources.

The following tables identify the specific amounts of the material misstatements and related effects on the financial statements:

Balance Sheet Restatements		Original 2015	Restated 2015	Misstatement
Liabilities:	(Note 4)			
Liabilities With the Public				
Accounts Payable		$ 410,663	$ 280,286	$ 130,377
Other:				
Accrued Funded Payroll and Leave		$ -	$ 155,268	$ (155,268)
Unfunded Leave		$ 340,544	$ 340,544	$ -
Total Liabilities		$ 752,445	$ 777,336	$ (24,891)
Net Position:			$	
Unexpended Appropriations - All Other Funds		$ 2,786,494	$ 2,761,603	$ 24,891
Cumulative Results of Operations - All Others		$ (151,509)	$ (151,509)	$ -
Total Net Position - All Other Funds		$ 2,634,985	$ 2,610,095	$ 24,891
Total Net Position		$ 2,634,985	$ 2,610,095	$ 24,891
Total Liabilities and Net Position		$ 3,387,430	$ 3,387,430	$ -

Statement of Net Cost Restatements

		Original 2015	Restated 2015	Misstatement
Gross Cost		9,472,592	9,741,850	(269,258)
Net Program Cost	(Note 5)	9,472,592	9,741,850	(269,258)
Net Cost of Operations		9,472,592	9,741,850	(269,258)

Statement of Budgetary Resources Restatement

STATUS OF BUDGETARY RESOURCES	Original 2015	Restated 2015	Misstatement
New obligations and upward adjustments	$ 9,785,568	$ 9,836,572	$ (51,004)
Apportioned	$ 129,676	$ 129,676	$ -
Unapportioned	$ 1,695,921	$ 1,644,917	$ 51,004
Unobligated balance brought forward, end of year	$ 1,825,597	$ 1,774,593	$ 51,004
Total budgetary resources	$11,611,165	$11,611,165	$ (0)
CHANGES IN OBLIGATED BALANCE			
Unpaid obligations, brought forward, October 1 (gross)	$ 2,155,844	$ 2,155,844	$ -
New obligations and upward adjustments	$ 9,785,568	$ 9,836,572	$ (51,004)
Outlays (gross) (-)	$ (9,836,743)	$ (9,836,743)	$ -
Recoveries of prior year unpaid obligations (-)	$ (731,870)	$ (731,870)	$ -
Unpaid obligations, end of year	$ 1,372,798	$ 1,423,802	$ (51,004)
Obligated balance, start of year (net)	$ 2,155,844	$ 2,155,844	$ -
Obligated balance, end of year (net)	$ 1,372,798	$ 1,423,802	$ (51,004)

Statement of Changes in Net Position Restatements

	Original 2015	Restated 2015	Misstatement
Budgetary Financing Sources:			
Appropriations used	9,393,368	9,418,258.36	(24,891)
Other Financing Sources (Non-Exchange):			
Imputed Financing Sources (Note 8)		244,367.53 $	(244,368)
Total Financing Sources	9,393,368	9,662,625.89	(269,258)
Net Cost of Operations	9,716,959	9,741,849.95	(24,891)
Net Change	(323,592)	(79,224.06)	(244,368)
Cumulative Results of Operations	(395,876)	(151,508.60)	(244,368)
Budgetary Financing Sources:			
Appropriations received	9,200,000	9,200,000.00	-
Other adjustments	(275,316)	(275,316.19)	-
Approprations used	(9,393,368)	(9,418,258.36)	24,891
Total Budgetary Financing Sources	(468,684)	(493,574.55)	24,891
Total Unexpended Appropropriations	2,786,494	2,761,603.31	24,891
Net Position	2,634,985	2,610,094.71	24,891

Section: IV: Other Accompanying Information

A. Summary of Financial Statement Audit and Management Assurances

Summary of Financial Statement Audit

Audit Opinion: Disclaimer
Restatement: No

Material Weaknesses	Beginning Balance	New	Resolved	Consolidated	Reassessed	Ending Balance
Total Material Weaknesses	1	0	0	0	0	1

Summary of Management Assurances

Effectiveness of Internal Control over Financial Reporting - Federal Managers' Financial Integrity Act (FMFIA) 2

Statement of Assurance: Disclaimer

Material Weaknesses	Beginning Balance	New	Resolved	Consolidated	Reassessed	Ending Balance
Total Material Weaknesses	1	0	0	0	0	1

Effectiveness of Internal Control over Operations - FMFIA 2

Statement of Assurance: Unqualified

Material Weaknesses	Beginning Balance	New	Resolved	Consolidated	Reassessed	Ending Balance
Total Material Weaknesses	0	0	0	0	0	0

Conformance with Financial Management System Requirements - FMFIA 4

Statement of Assurance: Systems Conform

Non-Conformance	Beginning Balance	New	Resolved	Consolidated	Reassessed	Ending Balance
Total Non-Conformance	0	0	0	0	0	0

B. Improper Payments Information Act Reporting Details

The Improper Payments Information Act (IPIA) of 2002, as amended by the Improper Payments Elimination and Recovery Act (IPERA) of 2010, requires agencies to review all programs and activities they administer, and identify those programs that are susceptible to significant erroneous payments. Significant erroneous payments are defined as annual erroneous payments in the program exceeding both $10 million and 2.5 percent or $100 million of total annual program payments.

Risk Assessment

Due to the Commission's mission and size, the Commission does not separate its mission into individual programs. We conducted a risk assessment for all relevant payments. The Commission evaluated the following risk factors: whether the program or activity was new to the agency; the complexity of the program; the volume of payments; how eligibility decisions are made; recent major changes in funding, authorities, practices, and procedures; the level and experience of personnel; and significant deficiencies in audit reports. The risk assessment determined that the risk of significant improper payments was low. Furthermore, since the Commission's total budget is less than the $10 million threshold for significant improper payments, it is virtually impossible for the Commission to have improper payments over $10 million. Based on the risk assessment, we determined that the Commission does not have significant improper payments.

Payment Recapture Audits

Section 2(H) of the Improper Payments Elimination and Recovery Act requires agencies to conduct payment recapture audits for each program and activity that expends $1 million or more annually if conducting such an audit is cost-effective. Since the Commission's payments as defined in OMB Circular A – 123, Appendix C exceed the $1 million threshold, we conducted a cost-benefit analysis for the entire agency. To determine if it was cost effective for the Commission to engage in a Payment Recapture Audit, we estimated improper payments, determined the anticipated collections, examined the costs of a recapture audit, and applied OMB's criteria to make a decision. Based on our analysis, we have determined that the costs of a payment recapture audit at the Commission would exceed the benefits. In accordance with OMB Circular A – 123, Appendix C, we provided with our analysis and notified them that we decided that a payment recapture audit is not cost-effective.

Improper Payment Reporting

The Commission had no duplicate payment in Fiscal Year 2016.

APPENDICES

FY 2016-2018 STRATEGIC GOALS AND OBJECTIVES

Led by eight commissioners,[3] the Staff Director, along with, our national and regional office staff of civil rights analysts, social scientists, attorneys, and our 51 state advisory committees will carry out our mission by continuing to improve the alignment of our program activities with the goals and objectives in our strategic plan. We will measure performance against established targets, and report on our challenges and successes.

Throughout our history, the Commission has worked towards fulfilling our Congressional mandate to serve as a bipartisan, fact-finding federal agency charged with making recommendations on civil rights issues that affect our nation. With this in mind, the Commission solicited the views of Commissioners, staff members and Congress to identify areas of strength and weakness within the Commission and its activities. This input served as a basis for drafting our strategic goals.

Key concerns identified throughout this process centered around the need for the Commission to: produce more data-driven reports; increase the public's accessibility to these reports; and, to efficiently integrate the SACs into the Commission's work both as a way to raise public awareness of the essential work that the Commission is doing, and as a way to leverage the state-level resources of our SACs to inform the Commission's work.

As we move towards implementing our new strategic plan, the Commission's goal is to incorporate our stakeholders' feedback into our efforts to shape the nation's civil rights debate through expanded research, information, and reports generated by agency program activities.

---

[3] Four commissioners are presidential appointees and four are congressional appointees; all serve six-year terms.

Strategic Goal A:

The Commission will function as an effective civil rights watchdog and conduct studies and issue publications on important issues of civil rights.

Objective	Strategies	Performance Measures
• Strengthen the quality and objectivity of the Commission's reports.	• Concentrate studies and research on national priorities.	• The Commission will hold at least three briefings and/or hearings each year.

Strategic Goal B:

The Commission will regularly provide new, objective information and analysis on civil rights issues.

Objective	Strategies	Performance Measures
• The Commission will regularly conduct original fact-finding and/or a novel statistical data review in a civil rights investigation.	• The Commission will include selection of an investigation as part of its annual project planning. • The Commission will strengthen employees' ability to conduct investigations.	• During its regular project planning process, the Commission will select one investigative project involving original fact-finding and/or statistical data reviews, either as a stand-alone project or in conjunction with a briefing or enforcement report. • Upon approval of an investigative project by the Commission, SACs may be solicited to aid the Commission in state and local fact gathering. • The Commission will train and/or cross-train designated employees on field interview techniques and statistical analysis.

71

Objective	Strategies	Performance Measures
• All Commission products will be prepared using standards that provide for maximum objectivity.	• The Commission will strengthen its information quality standards and other procedures regarding the process and review of agency products, as well as the implementation of such standards and procedures.	• The Commission will amend its Human Capital Plan to prioritize developing employee capacities in the areas of statistical analysis and complaint interviews. • By 2016, the Commission will conduct a review of existing information quality standards, administrative instructions, and other quality control and quality assurance guidelines to ensure its reporting maximizes objectivity.

STRATEGIC GOAL C:

The Commission will cooperate, where appropriate, with other federal agencies to apprise individuals of civil rights laws and policies and to raise public awareness of civil rights.

Objective	Strategies	Performance Measures
• Strengthen the Commission's position as a national clearinghouse for civil rights information.	• Measure and analyze web traffic data on the clearinghouse web page to identify top three civil rights areas of interest	• Yearly updates to the clearinghouse web page. • Review annually (FY) and update, as needed, the Uncle Sam publication, in both English and Spanish. • By FY 2016, issue quarterly data reports that

Objective	Strategies	Performance Measures
• Consult with the civil rights divisions of other agencies to ensure dissemination of accurate information for the complaint referral process.	• Maintain up to date information on the USCCR complaint referral process. • Simplify the telephone complaint referral process.	list and rank clearinghouse information hits tabulated by agency (DOJ, EEOC, DOE and DOL). • List the name, URL and contact information for each Federal Civil Rights division that we refer complaints to on the USCCR website. • Contact the Federal civil rights divisions that we refer complaints to, semi-annually, to confirm accuracy of civil rights complaint contact information. • By 2016 update the phone lines to allow callers to use a push button system to obtain complaint referral information (ex: push 1 for Employment; Push 2 for Housing, etc.)

STRATEGIC GOAL D:

Improve the Commission's profile and effectiveness in communicating with the general public.

Objective	Strategies	Performance Measures
• Raise public awareness of the Commission's work	• Expand Press Outreach	• Create and update press list on a regular basis • Issue press releases (English & Spanish) and update website prior to every hearing and briefing. • Participate in speaking engagements and public policy symposia.
• Modernize the Commission's information technology infrastructure to increase access to the Commission's work products. • Improve access to agency publications and dissemination of information for all persons including persons with disabilities and persons with limited English proficiency.	• Revise and reformat the website to increase web traffic and access to publications. • Increase access to Commission briefings and hearings using online tools • Measure and analyze web traffic and written requests for Commission reports. • Revise and update the USCCR website to make electronic and information technology (EIT) accessible to persons with disabilities.	• Reformat website to increase Google hits. • By FY 2016, Commission briefings and hearings will be streamed live online and made available on the website for future viewings. • By FY 2016, issue monthly reports on downloads and written requests for USCCR publications (top ten for each category). • By FY 2016, the agency shall implement accessible elements on the website, including alt tags, long descriptions,

Objective	Strategies	Performance Measures
• Expand and clarify the USCCR complaint process for all individuals including LEP persons and persons with disabilities.	• Analyze complaint line data and written requests for assistance to identify language access needs. • Improve web-based complaint screening process and online guidance to complainants.	and captions, as needed.[4] • By FY 2016, all documents on the website shall be made available in HTML or a text-based format.[5] • Maintain log (library and complaint line) to identify which language, other than English, is most often used by callers/writers when they contact the Commission. • By FY 2016, update the USCCR website to include direct links to federal agencies' civil rights complaint page.

---

[4] These elements are necessary in order to make web pages accessible for persons with disabilities.

[5] This format is necessary so that a person using a screen reader can access online documents or documents provided library on disc.

STRATEGIC GOAL E:

Continue to strengthen the Commission's financial and operational controls and advance the Commission's mission through management excellence, efficiency, and accountability.

Objective	Strategies	Performance Measures
• Continue to strengthen the Commission's financial, budget, and performance policy, procedures, and reports • Improve the strategic management of the Commission's human capital	• Align the Commission's budget submissions with the Agency's strategic plan and annual performance plan. • Ensure that the Commission's budget submission complies with OMB Circular A-11. • Enhance financial policy and procedures to ensure reliability of financial reporting. • Monitor and report on the Commission's progress in achieving its annual performance plan goals and objectives. • Update and Implement the Commission's Human Capital Plan to ensure the agency has a highly skilled and flexible workforce to carry out its mission.	• Compliance with OMB Circular A-11 • Compliance with OMB Circular A-11 • Receive a "clean" or unqualified financial statement audit. • Submit a Performance and Accountability Report that adheres to all relevant guidance. • Implementation of commission's and the Office of Personnel Management (OPM) Human capital Plan program, strategies and initiatives. • Results of the Employee Satisfaction surveys compared to previous surveys. • Annual training sessions, i.e., formal training,

Objective	Strategies	Performance Measures
• Improve administrative and clearinghouse services including information technology, acquisition, and library functions.	• Conduct and analyze Employee Satisfaction surveys and develop specific strategies to address issues. • Conduct training to increase awareness of acquisition processes and procedures. • Comply with Federal information security requirements. • Leverage information technology to enhance the productivity and efficiency of the workforce.	issuance of memoranda and/or internal instructions. • Annual FISMA audit • Comply with OMB Cloud Computing Initiatives.

STRATEGIC GOAL F:

Increase the participation of our State Advisory Committees (SACs) in the Commission's work.

Objective	Strategies	Performance Measures
• Include SAC input in the Commission's program planning process. • Enhance collaboration between and among SACs, regional offices and the Commission.	• Solicit SAC involvement in briefings and hearings. • Expand communication and information sharing	• By FY 2016, SACs will be encouraged to participate in at least two briefings/ hearings/fact-finding and/or public forums annually. • Issue monthly updates via listserv (from DC office to Regions).

Objective	Strategies	Performance Measures
	through the use of a listserv and webinar capabilities.	• By FY 2016, Regional offices will have the capability to offer webinars. • Extend SAC appointee terms to 4 years.
• Strengthen the SAC re-chartering process	• Achieve and maintain chartered status for all 51 SACs.	• Eliminate SAC backlog by FY 2016. • Re-charter SACs set to expire after 10/1/2016 within 60 days.

Appendix B: FY 2016 Annual Performance Plan, Targets, and Results

Strategic Goal A: The Commission will function as an effective civil rights watchdog and conduct studies and issue publications on important issues of civil rights.

Performance Measures	Performance Goals	FY 2016 Performance Target	FY 2016 Actual Performance
The Commission will hold at least three briefings and/or hearings each year.	3 briefings or hearings	3 briefings or hearings	Exceeded 4 briefings

Strategic Goal B: The Commission will regularly provide new, objective information and analysis on civil rights issues.

Performance Measures	Performance Goals	FY 2016 Performance Target	FY 2016 Actual Performance
During its regular project planning process, the Commission will select one investigative project involving original fact-finding and/or statistical data reviews, either as a stand-alone project or in conjunction with a briefing or enforcement report.	1 investigative project	1 investigative project	Met
Upon approval of an investigative project by the Commission, SACs may be solicited to aid the Commission in state and local fact gathering.	Obtain assistance from at least 3 SACs during an investigative project	3 SACs assisting in an investigation	Substantially Met
The Commission will train and/or cross-train designated employees on field interview techniques and statistical analysis.	Train at least 2 employees in field interview techniques and statistical analysis	2 Trained employees	Not Met
The Commission will amend its Human Capital Plan to prioritize developing employee capacities in the areas of statistical analysis and complaint interviews.	Update Human Capital Plan to emphasis statistical analysis and complaint interviews	Implement Human Capital Plan	Not Met
By 2016, the Commission will conduct a review of existing information quality standards, administrative instructions, and other quality control and quality assurance guidelines to ensure its reporting maximizes objectivity.	Complete review	Complete Review	Met

Strategic Goal C: The Commission will cooperate, where appropriate, with other federal agencies to apprise individuals of civil rights laws and policies and to raise public awareness of civil rights.

Performance Measures	Performance Goals	FY 2016 Performance Target	FY 2016 Actual Performance
Yearly updates to the clearinghouse web page.	Update clearinghouse web page at least once a year.	Update Clearinghouse Webpage	Not Met
Review annually (FY) and update, as needed, the Uncle Sam publication, in both English and Spanish.	Review Uncle Sam yearly and update as necessary.	Review and Update Uncle Sam	Met
By FY 2016, issue quarterly data reports that list and rank clearinghouse information hits tabulated by agency (DOJ, EEOC, DOE and DOL).	Issue quarterly data report by agency	N/A	N/A
List the name, URL and contact information for each Federal Civil Rights division that we refer complaints to on the USCCR website.	Update contact information once a year	Update contact information once a year	Not Met
Contact the Federal civil rights divisions that we refer complaints to, semi-annually, to confirm accuracy of civil rights complaint contact information.	Update Federal civil rights divisions contact information twice a year.	Update contact information	Met
By 2016 update the phone lines to allow callers to use a push button system to obtain complaint referral information (ex: push 1 for Employment; Push 2 for Housing, etc.)	Update phone lines for complaint referral	N/A	N/A

Strategic Goal D: Improve the Commission's profile and effectiveness in communicating with the general public

Performance Measures	Performance Goals	FY 2016 Performance Target	FY 2016 Actual Performance
Create and update press list on a regular basis.	Update press list	Update press list	Met
Issue press releases (English & Spanish) and update website prior to every hearing and briefing.	Issue press releases for all hearings and briefings	3 press releases	Met
Participate in speaking engagements and public symposia	Participate in 3 speaking engagements or public symposia	3 public speaking engagements or symposia	Met
Reformat website to increase Google hits.	Reformat webpage	N/A	N/A
By FY 2016, Commission briefings and hearings will be streamed live online and made available on the website for future viewings.	Stream 2 briefings and hearings online and maintain video on the agency's website	2 Online briefing and/or hearing	Not Met
By FY 2016, issue monthly reports on downloads and written requests for USCCR publications (top ten for each category).	12 Monthly Reports	Monthly Reports	Not Met

82

Strategic Goal D: Improve the Commission's profile and effectiveness in communicating with the general public

By FY 2016, the agency shall implement accessible elements on the website, including alt tags, long descriptions, and captions, as needed.	Website is Accessible to Persons with Disabilities	25 percent of Website is accessible	Met - New Items are Accessible
By FY 2016, all documents on the website shall be made available in HTML or a text-based format.	All documents on the agency website are available in HTML or text formats	25 percent of documents are in HTML or text based	Met - New Items are Accessible
Maintain log (library and complaint line) to identify which language, other than English, is most often used by callers/writers when they contact the Commission.	Log all library and complaint line calls to determine language of requester	Complaint log identifies language of request	Met
By FY 2016, update the USCCR website to include direct links to federal agencies civil rights complaint page.	Website contains links to federal agencies civil rights complaint page	Update Links to Federal Agencies' civil rights complaint page	Not Met

Strategic Goal E: Continue to strengthen the Commission's financial and operational controls and advance the Commission's mission through management excellence, efficiency, and accountability.

Performance Measures	Performance Goals	FY 2016 Performance Target	FY 2016 Actual Performance
Compliance with OMB Circular A-11	Budget is aligned with the Agency Strategic Plan	Budget is aligned with the Agency Strategic Plan	Met
Compliance with OMB Circular A-11	Budget is compliant with OMB Circular A-11	Budget is compliant with OMB Circular A-11	Met
Receive a "clean" or unqualified financial statement audit.	Unqualified Opinion on financial statement	Unqualified Opinion	Not Met
Submit a Performance and Accountability Report that adheres to all relevant guidance.	Performance and Accountability Report adheres to all relevant guidance.	Performance and Accountability Report (PAR) adheres to all relevant guidance.	Met
Implementation of commission's and the Office of Personnel Management (OPM) Human capital Plan program, strategies and initiatives.	The Commission's Human Capital Plan is updated and implemented	Implement Human Capital Plan	Met
Results of the Employee Satisfaction surveys compared to previous surveys.	Employee Satisfaction survey scores increase each year.	Increase response rate by 10%	Met

(Cont'd)

Strategic Goal E: Continue to strengthen the Commission's financial and operational controls and advance the Commission's mission through management excellence, efficiency, and accountability.

Annual training sessions, i.e., formal training, issuance of memoranda and/or internal instructions.	Perform acquisition training as required.	Conduct acquisition training	Not Met
Annual FISMA audit	FISMA Audit	FISMA Audit	Met
Comply with OMB Cloud Computing Initiatives.	Agency is in compliance with Cloud Computer Initiatives	Compliant with Cloud Computer Initiatives	Met

Strategic Goal F: Increase the participation of our State Advisory Committees (SACs) in the Commission's work.

Performance Measures	Performance Goals	FY 2016 Performance Target	FY 2016 Actual Performance
Subject to budget constraints, by FY 2016, SACs will be encouraged to participate in at least two briefings/ hearings/fact-finding and/or public forums annually.	SACs will participate in 2 hearings, briefings, fact-finding, and/or public forums	SACs participation in 2 hearings, briefings, fact-finding, and/or public forums	Met
Issue monthly updates via listserv (from DC office to Regions).	Staff director or RPCU issues monthly updates to Regional Offices	RPCU issues updates to Regional Offices and SACs	Met
By FY 2016, Regional offices will have the capability to offer webinars.	Regionals office have the capacity to offer webinars	All regional office can conduct webinars	Met
Extend SAC appointee terms to 4 years.	SAC appointee terms are 4 years	SAC appointee terms are 4 years	Met
Eliminate SAC backlog by FY 2016	SAC backlog eliminated	N/A	N/A
Re-Charter SACs set to expire after 10/1/2016 within 60 days	80 percent of SACs are chartered within 60 days	80 percent	Met

www.ingramcontent.com/pod-product-compliance
Lightning Source LLC
Chambersburg PA
CBHW081405280526

45788CB00009B/2990